*A spiritual
seeker finds*

Authentic Enlightenment

Vail Carruth

*Former teacher of
Transcendental Meditation*

AUTHENTIC ENLIGHTENMENT

© Copyright 2007 by Vail Carruth

This book is an update of *The Kiss of God*,
which is still available through Vail Carruth.

First Printing 2007, ISBN: 9780942507423
Library of Congress Control Number: 2007933988

To contact Vail Carruth directly:
Living Light
e-mail: vail@living-light.net
Website: http://www.living-light.net
P.O. Box 721, Lavaca, AR 72941-4949
Phone: 479-674-2766   Fax: 479-674-2766

Published by **Deeper Revelation Books**
Revealing "the deep things of God" (1 Cor. 2:10)

P.O. Box 4260
Cleveland, TN 37320-4260
Phone: 423-478-2843   Fax: 423-479-2980
www.deeperrevelationbooks.org

Orders from wholesalers and bookstores should be directed to Deeper Revelation Books. Please call for a listing of distribution outlets.

DEEP REST AND FULFILLMENT
Scriptural References

Through these He has given us his very great and precious promises, so that through them you may participate in the divine nature and escape the corruption in the world caused by evil desires (2 Peter 1:4 NIV).

Meditate within your heart upon your bed and be still (Psalm 4:4).

They looked unto Him, and were lightened, and their faces were not ashamed (Psalm 34:5 KJV).

Come to me, all you who labor and are heavy laden, and I will give you rest. Take My yoke upon you and learn from Me, for I am gentle and lowly in heart, and you will find rest for your souls. For My yoke is easy and My burden is light (Matthew 11:28-30).

There remains therefore a rest for the people of God. For he who has entered His rest has himself also ceased from his works as God did from His. Let us therefore be diligent to enter that rest... (Hebrews 4:9-11).

But those who wait on the LORD shall renew their strength; They shall mount up with wings like eagles; They shall run and not be weary, They shall walk and not faint (Isaiah 40:31).

But we all, with unveiled face, beholding as in a mirror the glory of the Lord, are being transformed into the same image from glory to glory, just as by the Spirit of the Lord (2 Corinthians 3:18).

But whoever listens to Me will dwell safely, and will be secure, without fear of evil (Proverbs 1:33).

And you will seek Me and find Me, when you search for Me with all your heart (Jeremiah 29:13).

FOREWORD

What is there about traditional religions that leave so many people bored and unsatisfied: Today, people everywhere are pursuing spirituality outside the confines of their churches in an effort to achieve personal fulfillment and authentic spiritual experience. It is this lack of fulfillment that drove Vail Carruth into the New Age, Eastern mystical paths to enlightenment and to transcendental meditation where she became a teacher of "TM." Her book, *Authentic Enlightenment*, is an engaging account of her experiences that may challenge your closely held beliefs. Proceed with caution but with great expectation because these insights could revolutionize your entire world view!

The strength of this book is its truthfulness. With unflinching candor, Vail takes the reader on a fascinating spiritual journey that runs the entire gamut from her experience with "recreational" drugs as an authentic counter-culture member of the 60's hippy movement, to TM, and finally to a discovery that was to change her life forever. In a surprising loop, Vail once again returned to her original faith but with a difference. She discovered God's love for her—the missing puzzle piece that the New Age movement could not deliver. In turn, she found that only by loving Jesus because of the finished work of the cross could she experience the fullness of God's love. It is the combination of God interacting with the cherished people he has created that gives life meaning.

We human beings were created to love God and to experience His love for us. Without experiencing this amazing love, we will never be complete or whole. Although Vail enjoyed some benefits of meditation, something was definitely missing. It would serve us well to seriously consider and question the end point of the particular path we are on before we follow it to its ultimate conclusion.

We cannot become complete or know the amazing joy and love of God, nor can we have legitimate and authentic, rich spiritual experience without being intimately connected to this Lover of our souls. Joined to Him, we can grow into all that we were designed to be. If anything can describe Vail's life and spiritual journey, it would be summarized in one phrase, "In pursuit of God." The chronicle of her journey, *Authentic Enlightenment*, is a must for anyone who is sincerely seeking genuine, rich spiritual experience based on the solid bedrock of truthfulness and reality. When people come to discover how much they are passionately loved by God as Vail did, when they experience for themselves the length and breadth, the height and depth of the power and love of God for them, they will also receive other benefits as well—spiritual, physical, and mental—that practices like TM attempt to deliver. And people will not have to meditate for hours and alter their consciousness for this glory to break out in their lives! All that is required is a humble, open heart and an honest hunger for truth. No one will be disappointed.

—Mike Bickle

Mike Bickle is the Director of the International House of Prayer of Kansas City, a 24-hour a day ministry of "Worship with Intercession" in the spirit of the Tabernacle of David which has continued without stopping in intercession and worship since September 19, 1999. He has authored several books including *Passion for Jesus, Growing the Prophetic* and *The Pleasures of Loving God*. Mike's teaching emphasizes how to grow in passion for Jesus. www.ihop.org

PREFACE

This world is a place of seeking. Human beings are constantly seeking after peace, joy, happiness, acceptance, fulfillment, security and most importantly, the path that leads to immortality. Such is a perfect description of Vail Carruth—the seeker. She was not satisfied with what society presented as the status quo. She was not satisfied with a life lived for selfish purposes. She was not satisfied with mere religion: its traditions, rituals, ceremonies and doctrines. Her deep desire was to go beyond the boundaries of the normal human experience to pursue a personal encounter with Ultimate Reality. In the Bible, God gave a promise to persons of such spiritual caliber— *"You will seek Me and find Me, when you search for me with ALL your heart"* (Jeremiah 29:14).

God certainly did not "author" all the steps Vail took in her spiritual quest, but He did predetermine to use those events to bring her to a place of understanding, a place of wholeness and a place of purpose. She learned valuable life-lessons that have empowered her to be a voice of truth to other seekers of this generation. Maybe, just maybe, that's why you have felt drawn to this book. Walk through this truth-gate by faith and you will find the True Light that lights every person who comes in this world.

—Mike Shreve

Mike Shreve has traveled worldwide teaching God's Word since 1971. He is the founder/director of Deeper Revelation Books and The True Light Project: an outreach focused on sharing the Gospel with followers of other world religions. He is also the author of *In Search of the True Light*, an in-depth comparison of over 20 world religions.

www.shreveministries.org
www.thetruelight.net

Contents

INTRODUCTION

It is my hope that this book will cause spiritual seekers to be careful when they set out on a quest for spiritual experience. Most of us mistakenly rely on our own limited or imperfect understanding in choosing what direction or path we will take in our life's journey. Failing that, we attempt to entrust our souls and spiritual destiny into the hands of a mere human being, which is folly. Only our Creator can lead us safely home. He designed us, and He has given us the Book of books for a faithful and true witness. Spiritual experiences without a firm knowledge of this book and a close, intimate relationship with God are insufficient barometers of spiritual attainment. It takes fearless honesty, not technique, to discover and understand His love. God has given to each of us a mustard seed of faith to find Him. You have to first "believe that He is, and that He is a rewarder of them that diligently seek Him" (Hebrews 11:6).

The presence of the Almighty suddenly crossed my path one day in response to a simple prayer. I found fulfillment, not by following the path I was on, but by getting off of it. God had something so much better for me. I believe my spiritual journey reveals that God in His great love for us is able to take us by the hand and lead us to the place of His righteousness, peace, and freedom that we both desire and desperately need.

I thought that by following certain spiritual practices, I would eventually reach enlightenment. But God is no respecter of persons. He'll come to you whether you are knowledgeable and sophisticated or you can barely tie your shoes. If you sincerely desire to know God and are truly sorry for having withstood His rightful leadership over your life, He will forgive and profoundly change you.

My life as a spiritual seeker and fringe member of the 60's hippie movement led to my involvement in Transcendental Meditation and New Age philosophy. This is a story of the wonderful grace, mercy, love, and power of God that took me beyond these popular mindsets into a real encounter with my heavenly Father. May it help light your own path to freedom.

1

The Open Ward

We have exchanged the glory of God for other things... The sun of God's glory was made to shine at the center of the solar system of our soul. And when it does, all the planets of our life are held in their proper orbit. But when the sun is displaced, everything flies apart. The healing of the soul begins by restoring the glory of God to its flaming, all-attracting place at the center.[1]

—*John Piper*

TUNE IN, TURN ON, DROP OUT

*B*erkeley in the 1960s was a place of great social ferment. Either you found your niche in this great living experiment ("The Open Ward" as some called it) or else you had the feeling that it was another planet and that you had best leave quickly. Vintage members of the 60's hippy movement, even fringe members like myself, felt there was no other place on earth its equal. Even those from the "far side" found in Berkeley a comfortable social acceptance. Many of us could feel stirrings of the winds of change gathering on the horizon. Perhaps you, too, have sensed its growing momentum.

There seemed to be two general divisions of the San Francisco-Berkeley Bay Area youth culture at the time: the political activists and the spiritual seekers. For the record, there was a third group from the university which the rest of us considered almost subhuman and detestable—the fraternity jocks, whose lifestyle exemplified what the rest of us practically villainized: materialism in the form of reckless spending, loud attention-getting beer parties, and what appeared to be a Neanderthal level of spiritual awareness.

There was an unspoken consensus among us that something was terribly wrong with the way things were going. The political activists thought they could remedy the world's problems by joining peace marches and student strikes or by serving jail time for confrontations with police. I personally preferred to observe the barbed wire and the tear gas from a safe distance.

Because of my artistic temperament, I opted for the non-political approach. Believing that what the world needed was a basic change in consciousness, my friends and I adopted the then popular motto, "Tune in, turn on, and drop out." People like us could be found taking LSD and smoking marijuana, going back to the land and joining communes, attending encounter groups, or simply meditating.

TWILIGHT ZONE

The first time I tried marijuana alone in my dorm room, I thought I had discovered a third state of mind—a twilight zone between waking and dreaming in which all dualities seemed to dissolve into a unified whole, or gestalt. This experience gave me a profound, but temporary, sense of freedom from guilt and fear and seemed to whet my appetite for more spiritual experiences. In order to maintain this euphoria, I learned to make hashish or marijuana brownies so I could get high inconspicuously. I soon graduated to other kinds of "mind expanding" hallucinogens, drugs such as LSD, peyote, mescaline, and even horse tranquilizers. Friends would offer "acid" to us claiming that it was "really pure stuff," but no one really knew its source or whether it was mixed with anything dangerous. Once I tried taking nutmeg, but the high didn't compensate for the serious headache that sent me to the doctor's office afterwards. Some of my LSD trips also had unpleasant "side effects," like the time a ten foot entity decided to show up and stood by my side for a long time. I never totally freaked out the way some of my friends did, but after one especially powerful LSD trip, I felt as though I had received a frontal lobotomy and was in a daze hardly able to think or speak for weeks afterwards.

After awhile, I lived in the famous Haight-Ashbury section of San Francisco, regularly visiting the Psychedelic Shop and attending the famous Bill Graham rock concerts, the Golden Gate Park Love Be-Ins, and the like. It was a time in my life when I felt that I could live out all my fantasies, just as long as they didn't collide with someone else's. It was cool first to get stoked up on acid and then arrive "high" at these Bill Graham concerts dressed in all kinds of far-out costumes. Driven by an attack of drug-induced craving for "munchies," my first order of the evening would be to head for the counter that was always laden with a tantalizing display of food and snacks. The music was so loud, however, that it hurt my ears, so I only went to a couple of these concerts. I realized that I might become deaf if I were to attend any more. In fact, a few of my friends became quite deaf as a result of regularly attending them.

I also realized that marijuana and LSD were affecting my memory. After hearing several horror stories about bad LSD trips, I gradually began to see that taking recreational drugs was like playing Russian roulette with my life and sanity. I came to believe that being high was something we should attain solely as a result of a healthy lifestyle.

Living among the hippies had at least one good point—they taught me the value of health food. There were a lot of great juice bars right on the street where you could buy freshly squeezed grape or carrot juice, which is very delicious and energizing. I still love fresh juices and I believe that they are some of the greatest healing substances on earth. However, many of my acquaintances in the counterculture believed that you could sort of "eat your way" to God. Health food is a great idea, but it has its limitations like everything else. The best it can do is to make you feel calmer and provide you with stamina to fight emotional distress.

Another good point about the hippies—they had it right about materialism, but some of them took it too far and developed a kind of reverse, elite snobbery toward anything "establishment." However, one can learn from overstatement. It is true that some people are imprisoned by their shortsightedness and can only see the world through a Bar Code. Materialism can blind you and divide your vision. It can also limit your freedom and keep you from receiving the light of revelation that can bring true transformation. But we human beings tend to resist change.

One day, a couple of my hippy friends went into my kitchen and declared almost everything as unfit to eat. In a short time I had completely switched over to brown rice, whole wheat bread, sprouts, lots of fruits and veggies (many of them raw), nuts, honey, and sea salt. But the Haight-Ashbury living experiment began to turn sour for me as reports of frequent thefts and even some murders began to surface. When the house next door was robbed by a cat burglar, I decide that it was time to move on.

How did a nice, well brought-up girl like myself, daughter of a prominent doctor and product of girls' finishing schools, wind up in rough and tumble Berkeley, pivotal spot of the 60's counterculture movement? To help you understand how I arrived there, I'd like to briefly take you back to my early roots.

2

Early Beginnings

PRINCETON

*T*he early years of my life were spent in the outskirts of Princeton, New Jersey and Erie, Pennsylvania. My first memories are of a large, white two-story house with an abundantly producing apple tree in the backyard alongside a strip of woods. We lived on a mini-farm, which included about fifteen hogs, some chickens, ducks, and a vegetable garden.

Our animals always provided us with a source of fun and fascination. It never ceased to amaze me how tirelessly our robot-like ducks would speed around the corner of the house for a hand out. Their level of expectation never seemed to waver, even when the snacks were not forthcoming. It's a tribute to the determination of the species that I was never able to wear them out, although a child's capacity for repetition can be formidable. I was motivated, not by benevolence, but by a desire to experiment with my power over them. Another favorite activity was playing "club house" with our neighborhood friends in a small, wooden shed that we used as a private hideaway.

Life with three brothers was not always an even battle. I declared to them that God was going to give me a baby sister, and I was right. Jessie was the fifth and last child, positioning me right in the middle.

Our seemingly idyllic life setting was shattered by the death of my father from kidney failure. Losing him at the tender age of five was very difficult for me, as we had been very close. To compound matters, this followed on the heels of World War II. I recall hearing the radio announcement of the bombing of Hiroshima and Nagasaki and listening to Mom and Dad discuss the news articles. The shock of my exposure to these events is probably what brought on my fear of trains. In the middle of the night, I would be awakened by the sound of the loud, insistent horn of a train as it sped through the New Jersey countryside. Terrified with the thought that it was heading straight toward me, I would run to my mom's bed for comfort. In the face of having to raise four children alone, Mother's strength and resilience must have been drawn from some deep, hidden reservoir.

After one terrifying train episode sent me running to the safety of her bed, she carried me out to the verandah to gaze at the night sky. It was a hot summer night, and as I looked up at the sky, I wondered if it perhaps held a promise of something more. But deep within its vast silence, it remained a closed canopy of darkness, studded by a scattering of stars. The next thing I knew it was morning, and I was back in my own bed.

Every night, the train would come right on schedule, evoking that same nameless fear. So I prayed and asked God to please make the train noise go away. Suddenly, the soothing sound of an airplane far up in the sky superseded the wail of the evil train, leaving in its wake a great stillness. This scenario occurred every night, giving me a feeling that *Someone* up there loved me and was answering prayers.

After my father's death, my mother married a successful surgeon who worked at Hammot Hospital, in Erie, Pennsylvania. My parents decided that California was a much better place to bring up children, so we moved to Saratoga where my new dad, Dr. August Jonas, became the chief surgeon at Kaiser Hospital in San Francisco.

CALIFORNIA

When our family car made its maiden voyage through Saratoga, California, orchards of luscious fruit trees passed by our windows. The West Coast grocery stores always abounded with many varieties of fresh produce, in contrast to the limited choices to which we were accustomed back east.

The happy Saratoga days ended with the death of my stepfather. He had been a remarkable man with a great heart to take on all of us kids, and his strong leadership and fine values left an indelible mark. He had made sure that we all attended church. Our Episcopal minister was a very dynamic and loving person who wanted us to have a personal relationship with Christ. But even though we went through "confirmation" classes, I do not recall a public invitation ever being extended to receive Jesus into my life as my personal Savior.

We had been attending private high schools because early on my mother had accurately observed the deteriorating moral and intellectual climate of the public schools. Finally, to facilitate our adjustment to life without a father and to make a new life for my mother, we moved to San Francisco near the cable car route and Chinatown. At that time, kids could safely explore downtown areas alone without their parents. San Francisco was just as colorful and exciting as we had imagined, although living there was entirely different from our former neighborhood. We loved riding up and down the city hills on cable cars. My favorite pastime was going to the stores in Chinatown, buying and nibbling on melon candy, and observing all the exotic things to eat displayed in the windows.

After several years in San Francisco, my mother married Ralph D. Bennett, former professor of electrical engineering at MIT and facilitator of the unique ship demagnetizer of mines used in World War II. Among his many other projects, he designed a way to preserve and store the beautiful old tapestries at the De Young Museum in San Francisco, where he and my mother worked for many years. Her expertise as docent and research writer for the museum's tapestry and other exhibits earned her international recognition. On the home front, our house was filled with many of Ralph's scientific "inventions" designed to expedite life's tedious chores, but I never understood all of them. Ralph was a good friend and a great and unusual man who lived a long and productive life.

3

Hints of Immortality

EARLY ROOTS

The outward drama of my early life was underscored by a deep, relentless hunger for personal identity. To fill in this part of my life's story, I must backtrack a little to my first spiritual awakening. My mother had already laid the foundation for my faith by frequently mentioning the gentleness and goodness of Jesus. I was fascinated every time she mentioned His name. At the age of 10, my grandmother gave me a book for my birthday, *The Princess and the Goblin* by George MacDonald. This book was not "preachy" and gave me a real appetite for good spiritual books. I could hardly put it down.

There was also a succession of kitchen helpers in our home, one of whom regularly listened to Christian radio programs, and I remember experiencing the presence of the Spirit of God while listening to them. Over time, several of these ladies shared their faith with us, so I increasingly came to realize God's love for me and His eternal provision through Christ.

When I was twelve years old, our kitchen helper took us to a summer camp church meeting. This was the first focused church outreach I had ever seen. It was at an Assembly of God church in Los Gatos, a small town near Saratoga.

When the invitation was given, I felt powerfully drawn to acknowledge Jesus as my Savior. At the time, I was not fully aware of all of the ramifications of being "born again." The acknowledgment of my faith was not accompanied by any "fireworks or signs." And no one ever brought us back to that church for follow-up or discipleship. My own church was probably unaware of what had happened to me (and I was clueless). From that point until I was about thirty years old, I drifted away from Jesus and more or less "did my own thing." Unfortunately, I am afraid this probably happens to many new believers who have no follow-up after their conversion.

My interest in spirituality, coupled with a lack of foundational undertanding of the Holy Scriptures, drew me toward some experiences that would later prove to be counterfeits of spiritual fulfillment. I justified the confusion and rebellion of my teen years by thinking that maybe I was more sensitive and creative than others and could embrace the supernatural. Unfamiliar with the dangers of trying to navigate spiritual waters without proper guidance, I began to experiment with the Ouija board, pendulums, astrology, hypnotism, and psychic phenomena. I even played games with my sister and brothers in which we would try to levitate tables and chairs with one finger by concentrating. I recall having a vivid, disturbing dream at this time that my body was being invaded by several different kinds of snakes that crawled up inside of me, but I didn't know what this meant. Snakes in dream interpretation language represent lies or deceptions. I also saw images of demonic faces. I knew that these were not ordinary dreams, and they left a deep impression on me. (I have realized that if young children are allowed to play with Ouija boards and indulge in these kinds of occult activities, they unknowingly could be inviting demonic influences into their lives.)

For the most part, our home was entirely free of occult books. However, one day I discovered a book on Hatha Yoga, possibly one of the many gifts given to my dad by patients. I used to stare at the pictures in this book with a kind of morbid fascination. It depicted a man cleaning out his sinuses with a string, sucking his stomach muscles in so far that he looked hollow, standing on his head, and getting into all kinds of contortions. I felt both strangely attracted and repulsed by these pictures. Another fascination was science fiction, sparked by seeing a movie called, "It Came From Outer Space," which was so frightening that it gave me nightmares for a long time afterward. I often listened to a radio program called "X Minus One," which featured stories from the strange shores of other worlds.

It wasn't long before I began to follow the guidelines of a book on developing psychic abilities. I set up an experiment in which a friend of mine picked a subject and then concentrated on it at the same time I tried to receive his impression. At the designated time just as I was about to fall asleep, I suddenly saw a clear image of a red rose. The next day he said that he had indeed concentrated on a red rose. When an acquaintance of mine was planning on betting on the horse races, I took a questionable leap of faith and boasted to him that I could predict which horses would win the race. He handed me a list of their names and thus began another psychic experiment. A few days later, he said that the horses I had picked did win.

Sometimes I would take a friend with me to visit a psychic, a palm reader, or a hypnotist. Afterward, we sometimes felt a spacey energy or presence that seemed to linger. These experiences aroused my curiosity and whetted my appetite for more than just a random "high." I wanted to "capture the fort," to go to the source of that spiritual power and learn how to remain in that state of consciousness permanently. *Although my desire for spiritual knowledge was legitimate, the groundwork was laid for a great snare and deception in my life.*

Lacking the kind of secure relationship with Christ that some of my friends seemed to have found, I was driven by a spiritual vacuum inside of me to search for a sense of identity and purpose. I enrolled in Lawrence College, a prestigious liberal arts school in Wisconsin, far away from my family and friends. At that time, the United States had come perilously close to nuclear war with Russia during the Cuban Missile Crisis, and I wanted to get away from big cities. My choice of college was partly motivated by a deep sense that someday there would be nuclear war on U.S. soil.

At Lawrence I experienced severe homesickness and then started having panic attacks, which became so bad that I could not eat. Determined to overcome this, I forced myself to face the dining room. Slowly the problem subsided, as my will overcame my paranoia. But a bad case of mononucleosis and hepatitis eventually forced me to leave the college. Two months of bed rest, megavitamins, and tender loving care from my mom enabled me to transfer to Northwestern University near Chicago.

The panic attacks resurfaced at Northwestern. My primary reason for transferring there was to be with my boyfriend, and when this relationship of three years broke up, the panic attacks grew much worse. I lost so much weight that I had to return home just to survive. The minute I did so, the panic attacks ceased until I transferred to the campus of the University of California, where it was "in" to be different. This was during the famous "Free Speech

Movement" of the early 60s. I managed to cloak my insecurities with a semi-hippy lifestyle and became involved with hallucinogenic drugs.

I was suffering from a state of purposelessness, meaningless living, and spiritual disintegration and didn't even know it. However, I think my parents partly understood where I was at spiritually, especially after they retrieved me from one LSD trip during which I had vomited all over the floor. At this time, I was reading a book that was very popular with the mind expansion crowd entitled _The Psychedelic Experience: A Manual Based on the Tibetan Book of the Dead._ During a peak LSD experience, I threw it out of the window because I realized that I didn't need to be reading a book of the dead but rather a book of the LIVING! But only God knew where I could find this _Book of Life._

As my interest and experience with altered states of consciousness grew, I explored the writings of Richard Alpert and Timothy Leary, former Harvard professors who had dropped out of the academic world to pursue the path of altered awareness. Leary emphasized psychedelics, whereas Alpert metamorphosed from hallucinogens to various spiritual paths and forms of meditation, becoming a sort of Western guru. I even attended their seminars on psychedelics at the University where I actually _studied_ how to get high. A group of Christians developed a pamphlet around one talk given by Leary. They challenged the idea that drugs could lead to enlightenment. However, they did not proselytize or try to convert us.

As I abandoned psychedelics, I filled in the gap with Eastern mystical pantheism. "Tripping" inevitably led to spiritual "dabbling," but I still had a severe case of fragmented identity. First, I began to explore the popular writings of Alan Watts and then Herman Hesse. I also consulted the *I Ching* and astrology. Swept along by this popular tide of eastern philosophy, I soon departed from my original Christian roots, and began to view myself as my own savior and destiny maker.

SPIRITUAL BUFFET

The occult epidemic of the 60s has widened and gradually infiltrated and merged with many aspects of today's society, producing many new philosophical hybrids and spiritual techniques. During the early days, I was drawn toward the paranormal because of studies in parapsychology that seemed to legitimize it as being scientific. I was aware of the psychic research at Duke University and the various "proven" experiments that they were conducting. The premise was that psychic powers were part of latent human potential and needed only to be developed. The intent was to open and widen the horizon of human possibilities, therefore, providing solutions to many of the current unsolved problems facing our civilization.

If you have ever visited California, especially the San Francisco Bay Area, you will agree that for decades it has been home for a plethora of spiritual and self-enlightenment groups. In the 60s, there were countless such groups within just a few square miles. You could try them on one by one like a suit of clothes. When the going got rough or boring, you could simply toss one away like an old banana peel and pick up another one. Some of these organizations offered methods that were intriguing, challenging, and often bizarre.

Encounter groups never seemed to challenge me, although I attended my share of them. One of the first methodologies I tried was Scientology, but I asked for a refund of my initial fee a week later. They sent my money back along with a note saying that I was now on their "black list," officially excommunicated from the Church of Scientology. They gave no reason for my dismissal other than my quitting. Later, they sent me a letter saying that I was "pardoned."

I visited the Hare Krishna devotees on the Berkeley campus and chanted along with them, partaking of their ritual meals, which they handed out liberally to bystanders. All of their food is offered up to their god, Krishna, and they believe that giving food out to people influences them spiritually. I really liked their cuisine. They served delicious fruit yogurt, little sweet sticky balls, and other things with curry and exotic flavors that I love.

While being constantly surrounded by Eastern influences, I could not pass by the Berkeley campus without encountering the street preachers as they stood and endlessly quoted the Bible in front of the student union. One of these preachers was a red haired, wiry, middle-aged man with missing front teeth, masses of freckles, and a cayenne pepper disposition. They called him Holy Hubert Lindsey. If you didn't know that the man was full of love and compassion, you might think that he was full of the opposite, so utterly consumed was he by a hatred for "sin." I often listened to him and asked questions, developing a kind of friendship with him. I discovered much later on that he had been the original "Alfalfa" in the *Our Gang* movies.

When I learned that Hubert had gotten his teeth knocked out by a political activist, a Black Panther, my respect for him really grew. Barely conscious and covered with blood, he had said to his attacker, "I'll love you until the end," and then passed out. Evidently, another Black Panther had come to his rescue, threatening his attacker if he laid one more finger on Lindsey. The man who defended him later took over his preaching spot at Sproul Plaza on the Berkeley campus. Many scores of Berkeley hippies and other folks were converted, evidently because Lindsey preached and prayed faithfully in the face of much hostility and opposition. Lindsey died years later after having suffered complications from his many injuries.

There was another outspoken and powerful street preacher named Robert who I personally saw lead many to Christ. One day he attended a meeting held by the guru Muktananda. When Robert first entered the room, Muktananda immediately invited him to come up front, showering him with praise and favor and calling him a "highly evolved person." This special accolade convinced Robert (though I doubt he needed much convincing) to become a close disciple of Muktananda. Obviously, the desire for self-exaltation caused him to ignore or discard some of the exclusive Biblical concepts he had previously embraced.

COMPROMISE

During my first few years in Berkeley, I became involved romantically with a fellow named Rick that I had met in the Student Union Building. I took an immediate liking to him. He was tall, dark, and looked somewhat like Olive Oyle's Bluto. (Some have said that I look like Olive Oyle, but please don't *ever* tell me this.) With an IQ of 175, he had a Ph.D. in Physics and was a member of Mensa. He believed fervently that someday robots, programmed with artificial intelligence, would be able to replace human beings in almost every sphere of endeavor. I didn't approve of that idea, nor did I believe it would ever happen. If it did, I felt sure it would signal the end of the human race.

After dating Rick for about three years, it became apparent that he never wanted to get married or have children. On the other hand, I wanted very much to be married, so this frustrated me greatly. Rick somehow was able to convince me that marriage is old-fashioned, and that all married women become discontented once they are no longer single. For the sake of our relationship I tolerated the situation, but deep down in my heart it troubled me because I remembered the stable home life I had experienced as a child. I compromised my values and hid the pain, but this conflict became a self-imposed prison with far-reaching consequences. I discovered much later that the price of self-deception is always more than we anticipate. By faithfully following the light of truth that we know, we can eventually find the true spiritual breakthrough we are seeking.

Like many of my friends, I practiced birth control through Planned Parenthood for five years. Taking the pill for so long upset my hormones. When I stopped taking them, the abrupt hormonal change could have won me the title of "Zit Queen." The hormonal imbalance caused a systemic blood infection and fungal proliferation for years to come. Once I thought I might have been pregnant and took a pregnancy test, which came back negative, to my great relief. However, I would not have had an abortion had it been positive because I have never felt comfortable with the idea of killing any living person. For me, the painful lessons I have learned from my mistakes have been stepping stones to freedom. However, God's ways are universally unchangeable, and we do reap what we sow. I paid a price for this lack of integrity, evidenced by long-standing health problems that kept me from all that I wanted to accomplish. But thankfully, I did not have to remain in that quagmire forever.

During my relationship with Rick, I was introduced to the writings of Gurdjieff and Ouspensky, and went to several of the meetings held by followers of these teachers. But Rick would never discuss with me the hidden teachings. One concept I gleaned from reading Gurdjieff's books was that most people are "unconscious" or "asleep." I just was not convinced that Gurdjieff's way offered a worthy alternative. Rick and I took several LSD trips together and smoked pot frequently. One day during a peak LSD experience, I got what I felt at the time was a brilliant revelation. In dead seriousness, I announced to Rick that the most humble thing that I could say was, "I am God." He felt the same way about himself. It seemed as though we had hit upon a momentous truth.

One day we struck up a conversation with a very interesting looking person at the student union lunchroom. Eventually, our conversation swung around to our favorite topic—New Age philosophy and Eastern religion. To our surprise and disappointment, this very refined and knowledgeable person stoically refused to discuss it, saying that he followed Judeo-Christian beliefs and would not even consider anything occult. We ran into this man a number of times, once at a great little Indian restaurant on Telegraph Avenue where he was enthusiastically conversing with another friend about the virtues of health food. Though I see it differently now, back then Rick and I agreed that it was a tremendous waste of human potential that he was so spiritually narrow-minded. We felt really sorry for him and were appalled at how such an intelligent person could be so totally blind and shut off from other paths to enlightenment. It seemed that he had broken some unspoken rule.

Eventually it became very clear to me that my relationship with Rick was going nowhere, especially when he began dating another woman on the side. Sometimes he would invite her over to his house while I was there. He tried to convince me that I should be more "open-minded" and less "possessive." This was the final straw in what was a relationship that never should have been, and so I ended it with a great sense of relief.

A CHOICE DEFERRED

I've noticed that often just before we make a major wrong decision, we will be presented with a better choice, a "way out." I think that God wants to spare us from having to travel through unnecessary dark labyrinths like the one I was about to experience. God demonstrated His faithfulness and love to me by offering me another way. I discovered that two of my acquaintances from college dormitory days were living upstairs in my apartment building. Around their dinner table one day, they told me how they had come to experience a relationship with the living, resurrected Jesus Christ. They emphasized how His love had changed their lives amazingly, giving them indescribable happiness and peace. They seemed to be in a kind of Christian nirvana, and yet they were very grounded and real (not spaced out). They gave me a book to read about Israel's Six Day War and how God had miraculously intervened for that tiny nation.

Following their suggestion, I tried to read my Bible again, but they should have told me not to start at Genesis. As I had done in all my former unsuccessful attempts to read the Bible, I began at Genesis, once again getting stuck in the "begets." It might have made a big difference if I had started with the Gospel of John. After reading the New Testament, I probably would have understood the Old Testament as well. But the Christian life did not match my mindset at that time, and I was not ready to trust Christ exclusively as they had done. So the Bible remained a closed book for me.

Soon after getting reconnected with my friends, I had an unusual experience. I had taken a secretarial job with Kelly Services as a typist in an office where several other women worked. One of them was none other than the former personal secretary of Billy Graham. The men in the office relentlessly teased her because of her stand on morality, but their taunts rolled off her like water from a duck's back and never swayed her beliefs. When she and I went out together for lunch, I asked her many questions. Though I confessed Jesus as my Savior, she seemed to sense (and I knew in my heart) that I did not really know Him in any real way.

One day, I met my two Christian friends coming down the stairs in the apartment building, and I told them that I was working in the same office as Billy Graham's former secretary. They grew very excited and told me that she was one of their best friends. I was amazed at this coincidence, and although they could see the hand of Jesus reaching out to me, I still had not met Him!

Meanwhile, all was not benign in that apartment building. Though my friends felt that God was trying to reach me, so was someone else. Up on the third floor lived a Satanist witch. She didn't wear a pointed black hat, but she had two black cats living with her. She told me that she regularly attended Anton LaVey's satanic church in San Francisco. She gave me a copy of her satanic bible to read. Now I had a choice between two competing bibles. The first seemed too boring, and the second too "bizarre," so I decided not to read either of them. Actually, there was a third one, if you include the *Essene Gospel of Peace* that I used to try to read at the Shambala bookstore on Telegraph

Avenue. Next to all the other exotic occult books, it seemed very bland and not very authentic.

In the apartment next to the Satan worshipper lived a Jewish couple. They complained that she cast spells and hexes against them out by their window fire escape, leaving evidence in the form of voodoo dolls with stuck pins and little piles of broken sticks. I felt that the witch was just being superstitious and venting her personal animosity, and I still refused to acknowledge the reality of an evil power. As far as my own philosophy went, I believed, "Do your own thing and let me do mine, if it doesn't hurt anybody." I blamed intolerance more than fallen human nature for the world's problems. (The recent wave of political correctness was enjoying its infancy during the countercultural days of the 60s.)

Telegraph Avenue was the hub of Berkeley's cultural life for us. There I joined many other street artists in peddling my art and jewelry. Years later, when I returned for a visit to Berkeley, I was advised that it was too dangerous to walk on Telegraph Avenue alone after dark unless escorted by the police. The amorality and so-called "freedom" of the 60s had morphed into a growing instability and lawlessness that infected the whole street area.

It was common on Telegraph Avenue to heckle Christians. At times an enormous golden idol was carried down the middle of Telegraph Avenue on a pull-cart among the dancing Hare Krishna devotees, the hawkers, and peddlers. Of course, the idol posed no threat to the Christians because it was only a statue, but the taunters seemed to derive intense satisfaction from parading it. They would yell, "The lions are hungry, Christians!" The Bible says that idols have eyes but don't see, and ears but don't hear, and that those who make idols become just like them—spiritually deaf and blind. (Actually, an idol can be anything that a human being loves and exalts more than his Creator.)

At this time, I could have had the wisdom of the ages given to me by our great and loving God, but all I could see was my own agenda. Faith would have unlocked the golden door to the incredible richness spoken of in Matthew 13:16-17: *"But blessed are your eyes for they see, and your ears for they hear; for assuredly, I say to you that many prophets and righteous men desired to see what you see, and did not see it, and to hear what you hear, and did not hear it."* Instead, my friends and I floated on the world's sea of universalism, disavowing moral and religious absolutes, and becoming hardened to Christianity in general. Looking out from behind our self-imposed barriers, we would often join in with the mockers of those who were enjoying their liberty on the narrow path to freedom.

However, since we were not full-fledged hippies, there was a tacit agreement among us to retain at least some sense of social responsibility and decency—the legacy from our parents. That's why I never sold out completely to hippiedom; it would have seemed grossly disloyal. Over the years I have had many occasions to be thankful for my "straight" upbringing. My Berkeley days more than confirmed the value of that upbringing. One time a friend of mine and I were driving down University Avenue, the main artery to the campus. The traffic was crawling along very slowly. As we looked to our left just off of the pavement, we witnessed a couple involved in such immorality we felt we needed to report it to the police. No one even seemed to notice, so I drove around the block and back to the scene just to make sure it wasn't a mirage. We left because we did not want newspaper reporters questioning us. Even then, social disintegration (now much further advanced) was clearly underway.

4

Maharishi Moves West

BACKGROUND

Transcendental Meditation (TM) hit the Berkeley campus in 1967 with its promise of relaxation and heightened awareness without the use of drugs. Meditation quickly became a household word. No longer the difficult austere discipline requiring hours of concentration and change of lifestyle, TM's mass appeal was its easy accommodation to the tempo of modern life. Surrounded by posters advertising a five-year plan to "Bliss Consciousness," students everywhere took the bait. For me, TM promised to fill the gap that all the accouterments of education and a high standard of living had not satisfied. Neither had the vagaries of an undisciplined life brought me any closer to knowing who I was.

Transcendental Meditation is actually a modern adaptation and offshoot of Eastern Hinduism. The late Maharishi Mahesh Yogi, founder of the movement, was born in India. He studied physics at Allahabad University and later became a close disciple of Swami Brahmananda Saraswati, or "Guru Dev" (which means divine teacher). Guru Dev was recognized as a powerful and holy member of the Shankara tradition of Vedantic Hinduism. It was during this close relationship with Guru Dev that

Maharishi mastered the Yogic technique, which he later simplified and popularized for Western consumption.

Maharishi meditated in a cave located in the Himalayas for two years. He was hoping to be well received in southern India because of his association with his master, but the people in India, long familiar with TM, were not impressed. However, it took spiritually confused America and Western Europe by storm. Maharishi, being a shrewd businessman, discerned that Westerners are in the habit of accepting things quickly.

Although he began to introduce TM to the West using the classical, spiritual approach, Maharishi ran up against some brick walls. First of all, he found that the West was steeped in materialism, and that most people were tired of "religion." With a strategy to reach the masses, he maneuvered around the Constitution's church/state separation clause by seeking scientific validation and governmental approval. Hence, there was a push to have TM taught in the schools under the title of the "Science of Creative Intelligence."

Like most people, I was unaware of the deceptive way TM was being presented and thought it would help me get my life more together. The Beatles had given TM some advance publicity, having practiced and studied TM in India under Maharishi. Taking our cue from the posters prominently placed on the Berkeley campus, my friends and I attended the two convincing introductory lectures by Maharishi's close associate, the very personable and magnetic Jerry Jarvis.

One of the intriguing things about TM was the promise that it could unlock the unused 90% potential of the brain. To think that I could finally balance the score between the gifted right side of my brain with the poor shriveled, logically challenged left side caused something inside of me to leap with joy. In addition to the prospect of developing a super brain was the possibility of other impressive "scientifically validated" benefits such as deep rest, self-awareness, creativity, and a sense of well-being.

THE HIDDEN MANTRA

The magic vehicle for this timeless travel experience was the amazing mantra, described as a "meaningless Sanskrit sound." Once you received your mantra, you were never to reveal it to anyone else. Your own personal word supposedly derived its power through hidden resonance, as if it needed to cringe from the light of day. To verbally announce your secret Sanskrit word would somehow weaken its effect by bringing it out of the subtle regions of the mind into the grosser (less subtle) levels of everyday life. Furthermore, we were told that the "purity" and "power" of the ancient teaching would be compromised or distorted, if uncovered.

At the first lecture, Jerry compared meditation to diving down in a submarine from the least subtle level of wakefulness to the deepest source of all thought, or "pure transcendental awareness." He likened this level to the ocean floor, which represented a state of no thought. The return trip back to the "surface" would supposedly bring renewed energy and creative intelligence into the affairs of daily life. How you could get something out of nothing I never could figure out.

He also compared TM to taking a jet plane, describing other forms of meditation as similar to riding a mule. Supposedly, TM would take you there faster and more comfortably, requiring much less effort. Of course, the fact that it was easy and quick appealed to everyone. The methodology that was presented went like this: Don't try to hold onto the mantra or to concentrate on it. Just repeat it silently until it slips from your conscious attention. Don't worry, as easily as you let it go, you will pick it up again. As your mind inevitably repeats these sounds, you begin to attain increasingly subtler levels of thought until you reach that ocean floor expanse of no thought, or "transcendental pure awareness." But that's only the beginning of the TM journey to cosmic consciousness.

JET AGE SPIRITUALITY

Even though I was skeptical at first, I found myself fascinated by the many analogies used to describe TM. With one of Jerry's famous, laid-back, benign grins, he echoed Maharishi, "Transcendental Meditation is the technique of the jet age." It seemed clear that the jet plane or submarine was taking us somewhere, but at first it wasn't clear exactly where. Unless it's a "magical mystery tour," most people appreciate knowing where they are going before heading out.

If people liked what they were hearing at the first introductory lecture, they were invited to come back to hear the rest of it. During the second lecture, it was revealed that the regular practice of Transcendental Meditation eventually would land the meditator in cosmic-consciousness. This promised state of cosmic-consciousness would continue whether awake or asleep. And then, of course, there were the two states of consciousness beyond cosmic-consciousness: God-consciousness and unity-consciousness. It was just assumed without question that these states of mind were desirable, and that everyone would want to "go there." It seemed all right with me then, but I did not know what I know now.

The lectures never hinted that TM might cause the following changes: 1) having your closely held religious beliefs subtly manipulated, influenced, and conditioned beyond recognition; 2) finding yourself face to face with uninvited apparitions and spirit visitors; 3) finding your sense of personal identity dissolving and becoming permanently lost in a huge "ocean of cosmic being," promoted as the final destination of this earthly journey. The emphasis was only that one would simply begin to lead a stress-free life, which seemed innocent enough to many participants.

PUJA INITIATION CEREMONY

The initiation ceremony following the first two lectures was a required procedure in learning TM. You simply would not be taught to meditate without it. There is a reason for this as I was to discover later when I became a teacher of TM. Witnessing the _Puja_ was required in order to prepare the "soil" (the person's soul) to receive the implanting of the "seed" (the mantra). In other words, it was supposed to establish the psychic condition in which the mantra would be effective. Maharishi acknowledged that something more than science is involved in the transfer of the mantra: "The entire knowledge of the mantras or hymns of the Vedas is devoted to man's connection, to man's communication with the _higher beings_ in different strata of creation "[2] (emphasis added).

After waiting seven hours in line, feeling tired and foolish holding my "offering" of a clean white handkerchief, three pieces of sweet fruit, and several wilting flowers, and paying the fee of $35, Jerry Jarvis personally took us through the first TM session. (Today, both beginning and advanced mantras now cost a whopping $1,200, and there are six or more advanced techniques. It is estimated that with the many "Age of Enlightenment" techniques and courses, "levitation" training, plus the myriad of various astrological and Vedic-based consultations, the eventual cost per participant can run as much as $100,000!)

Before we could be initiated into TM, we first had to remove our shoes, a ritual which made me consider the possibility of having to walk home barefoot. This procedure became second nature to me later during my many return visits to the meditation center as meditator, checker, and finally as TM teacher. I was led into a small candlelit room and offered a seat. After lighting some incense, Jerry placed my handkerchief, fruit, and flowers upon an altar in front of a framed picture of Guru Dev, the departed master of Maharishi. On the altar was also an assortment of devotional paraphernalia including rice, sandalwood paste, incense, water, and a polished set of brass utensils on a tray. Then Jerry sang the entire *Puja*, a Hindu song of praise and worship. I found myself wondering about the content since it was sung entirely in Sanskrit. During the introductory lectures, we had been told not to take any recreational drugs (marijuana, LSD, etc.) or medications not prescribed by our doctor. This was to ensure that the effects of our first meditation experience would be clearly attributed to TM and not to the drugs. Many concur that it is hard to tell the difference.

The *Puja* as a religious ceremony is designed to create a soul tie between the initiate and the departed Guru Dev. Although the teachers say the initiate is not involved with the ceremony, it is obvious that is not the case. When the *Puja* was finished, Jerry motioned with his hand for me to stand next to him while he concluded the ceremony in Sanskrit. Then he invited me to kneel down beside him.

My curiosity overruled my annoyance at this overtly religious display used to impart a supposedly scientific technique. During a few moments of silence, Jerry repeated my mantra, "ing," and had me repeat it a few times.

"Close your eyes and repeat it to yourself in your mind," Jerry said. As I began repeating the mantra silently, I felt that I was sinking down, down into a very quiet, dark place. After a moment, Jerry's voice broke the silence, "It is easy, no?" Then, "Open the eyes. Did you enjoy meditating?" I told him that I felt a little dizzy. After this he ushered me into another room where I was told to meditate for about 20 minutes. At the end of that time, I heard someone enter the room and quietly sit down near me. "Slowly open the eyes," he said. I gradually opened my eyes and then was directed to a room with a long table, where I filled out a questionnaire. There were questions such as, "Did you have any thoughts?" "Did you have any difficulty meditating?" "Did you try to force the mantra?"

When my friends and I left the TM center (with our shoes on), we acted and felt very giddy, laughing off and on for about three days. Wow! TM had really altered my consciousness! I always knew that someday I would find a way to get high naturally. I soon lost all interest in smoking pot because that only brought me "down" from my TM. Although I enjoyed this good feeling, I discovered later that it would come with a price greater than I was willing to pay.

As a follow-up to our initiation, we had to go to three nights of "checking" at the TM center to make sure we felt comfortable with our meditations and so they could answer any questions we might have. Some people wanted to know how the initiators knew what mantra to give people. There were many questions that seemed to go on and on and on into the night: "How could we be sure we were actually 'transcending?'" "What happens if you fall asleep when you are meditating?" "What if we were given the wrong mantra?" and so on.

The little children who had come along with their parents to receive their "walking mantras" (a word they can meditate on while they are up and about) eventually displayed unusual behavior. They didn't act happy and carefree as most children. Instead, they tended to be serious, quiet, and odd. It seemed as though a valuable part of their childhood had been stolen from them. Something in me balked at the idea of implanting a powerful mind-altering device (mantra) in the minds of innocent children.

CONDITIONING PROCESS

The idea that TM permanently conditions the nervous system and will change the very way one perceives reality is a far cry from the advertised claim that TM is only a simple technique of relaxation. In Maharishi's writings, he admits that practicing TM is a conditioning process. He describes how the first of the three goals of meditation—cosmic consciousness—is achieved:

> This (state) is brought about by regularly interrupting the constant activity of the waking state of consciousness with periods of silence in transcendental consciousness (via TM). When, through this practice, the nervous system has been permanently conditioned to maintain these two states together, then the consciousness remains always centered in the Self (emphasis added).[3]

The change of normal perception that results from this conditioning process may offer at least one explanation as to the willful misrepresentation about the religious nature of TM. Were the TM leaders intentionally deceptive—or were they themselves deceived, victims of the same conditioning, making it difficult or impossible for them to distinguish between truth and falsehood? ("I can't see the flies in my eyes because there are flies in my eyes.")

In a sworn and signed affidavit, a world-renowned expert on religious movements testified that Robert Winquist, then a member of the staff of Maharishi International University (MIU), had frankly confided to him: *"We don't mention the religious aspects because of public relations reasons. We are not downplaying TM as a religion; we are just not talking about it."* [4]

It is the very purpose of mantric meditation to alter the mental state of the meditator. I didn't realize that this conditioning process would alter my perception of the world until I began to believe the Hindu monist belief that "all is one" (i.e., I am God, the tree is God, my cat is God, as well as the energy all around me). As I progressed in TM, even the trees seemed to me to be alive with divine energy and appeared to have "spirits."

Paradigm Shift

A BREAK WITH TRADITION

*A*fter a couple of months of relatively smooth sailing, I started to encounter a few minor problems with my meditations. I felt very tired and edgy and sometimes had headaches. My meditations did not seem to flow along as they had at first, so I went to the TM center to have my meditation checked.

As I walked into the TM center, I was met by my checker, a strange emaciated girl with an unearthly pallor who seemed to lack any trace of personality. I noticed this paleness in a lot of those higher up in the TM ranks. Perhaps it was from meditating too long in the depths of the "ocean of consciousness." I soon began to view it as status symbol, but the weirdness still bothered me.

We sat down in one of the small meditation rooms for my checking session, and she answered my questions in a polite, expressionless manner. I was told to notice how effortlessly thoughts come and go and to think of the mantra just as effortlessly. For whatever reason (maybe it was the atmosphere of the place), this session of meditation was surprisingly deep and easy for me. I returned at other times for this checking procedure, but each time I could not get over thinking there was something mindless about it all.

Indeed, by my third checking session, I started to detect even stranger behaviors. Most of the TM teachers and checkers all spoke with the same lilting voice as Maharishi did. What's more, they all seemed to be in a very strange space, as if in a time warp, with their brains on hold. I'm not trying to be unkind; it just seemed that way. Unfortunately, the strangeness seemed to be catching. One day while I was in a clothing store purchasing a blouse, I was having difficulty carrying on a normal conversation with the sales lady. I attributed this to my feeling that I was becoming a very special, highly evolved person, and that it didn't seem worth my effort to try to relate to anyone on such a low level of consciousness. After mumbling a few words and paying for my blouse, I started walking slowly out of the shop when I distinctly heard the sales lady saying to her co-worker, "She's really strange." This comment should have bothered me, as usually I was alert to criticism, but it just confirmed to me that we were on different levels, mine of course being the higher.

Another example of this aloofness from normal human contact occurred at my mother's house, when an old friend of the family stopped in to visit us. It was Christmas time, and we were all sitting around the living room fireplace, enjoying the warmth of the holiday season. When this family friend reached out to me, I found myself declining to respond because I felt that her polite conversation was so unreal that it didn't deserve a reply. It was as though I functioned as two different people. One me realized I was being a pure snob, while the other me just looked on with complete detachment. I clinically observed her shock, her quickly stifled anger, and her cool rebuff as she turned her back to me and resumed talking with my mother.

In my apartment I was often aloof toward my two non-meditating roommates, passing them in the hallway without a word of acknowledgment. My attitude convinced them never to become meditators. The scary thing was that, at times, _I no longer seemed to be in control of my behavior._ Something _else_ was in control. I realized that it was a result of TM, but I was unwilling to stop meditating.

No wonder my mother found it difficult to understand me at that time. I recall writing what I felt to be a really revolutionary, bold letter to the mother of one of my brother's girlfriends. This parent seemed really cool because she was older, yet she still had young values—i.e., she was hip, artistic, and intellectual. I was sure that she would resonate with my ideas. She never wrote back.

In my letter to her, I wrote how I no longer enjoyed symphonic and classical music that were created along the usual Western pattern of development, climax and resolution. For me, this was moody music that was trying to "go" somewhere. Instead, my new musical taste reflected my feeling that life was more like the drone of a sitar, steady and hypnotic, without purpose, direction, or heroism.

As far as literature was concerned, I found myself losing the desire, even the capacity, to read. The only books I made an effort to read were about Eastern mysticism and the occult. Any kind of linear or directional thinking was difficult for me to sustain. I found myself becoming intolerant toward Western logic and proud to break with tradition. No matter that centuries of great art and literature, produced by the geniuses of our civilization, had won the devotion and appreciation of millions of people with discernment and taste down through the ages. It made no difference to me that my focus was narrowing down, funnel-like, to the reference point of only myself.

This new antisocial behavior of mine didn't endear me to people. But as the saying goes, "If you can't lick 'em, join 'em." TM teachers and checkers were a unique breed and regarded with admiration and a certain kind of awe by the regular TM meditating herd. Congregating by themselves, they did not like to mix with the lower echelons. So, in order to join the ranks of the special TM "elite," I decided that I would become a checker one day.

MOVING HIGHER

As I progressed in my practice of TM, I became quite "evangelical." One reason TM appealed to me was the concept of bringing peace to the world, one person at a time. I realized that it had to start with me. People finding inner peace would eventually solve the problem of wars, riots, and human unhappiness. This was actually a legitimate and noble idea. After all, I reasoned, Jesus referred to the Kingdom of God as being "within you." So I became very active in sharing TM (though hardly the Kingdom of God) with as many people as I could. My main reason for practicing TM was the promise that it would eventually lead me to peace and self-enlightenment, and finally to God. However, my concept of God was going through a radical transformation, reflecting something quite different from the personal Judeo-Christian God of the Bible.

One day at the women's gym, I struck up a conversation with a portly black woman as she was lifting some weights. With the sole intention of proselytizing for TM, I mentioned how great TM is and how the practice of TM can lead one to God-consciousness. This woman wasted no time in responding. Armed with a seemingly boundless love, she said that we do need God, and that *faith in God* is all that we need to know Him.

It was as though someone had struck me with a velvet glove right in the face. There was nothing more I could say. What can you say against faith in our Creator? This well-aimed arrow directly found the gap in my armor, which was my lack of trust in God. She evidently had faith in *her* Creator, and what's more, I could see that she had personal, confident knowledge of Him. TM had never given me that. Instead, TM's goal was to eliminate any acknowledgement of a personal relationship with the Heavenly Father and to dissolve the soul in an amorphous ocean of being. Embarrassed and with nothing to contribute, I turned and went on with my exercising, but another support had been removed from the false foundation on which I stood.

People's lives sometimes change gradually after a slow erosion of beliefs, one incident at a time. My everyday life as a TM teacher kept me well entertained and fascinated. Jerry Jarvis and Charley Lutes were everyone's favorite leaders in the movement. However, it was said that Charley, operating out of the southern California area, would frankly divulge unmentionable material about the weirder aspects of TM and other dark secrets, whereas Jerry stuck more to the straight, publicly presentable party line. Charley had been one of Maharishi's first Western converts. He held such positions in the movement as president of the Spiritual Regeneration Movement (TM's first organization in the West), and later as a trustee of Maharishi International University (now Maharishi University of Management.) It was rumored that Charley would sometimes mention UFOs, stating that they would someday land, and if you weren't spiritually "attuned," you might board the wrong saucer. (Evidently, there were two kinds of flying saucers—one benign and the other not so nice, although I don't think he went into great detail about what would happen if you made the wrong choice.) Charley even admitted that mantras were the "favorite names of the gods." Far-out questions about TM were always addressed to him. I secretly envied those from southern California, because Charley was their man, and they received more of the juicy tidbits. But I felt that it was extremely good karma to have been personally initiated by Jerry Jarvis, whom I genuinely liked.

For a year and a half, I studied piano at the San Francisco Conservatory of Music. Another student and I rented a small houseboat in a nearby town called Larkspur. The houseboat had a stained glass window and a huge grand piano in my studio bedroom, where I maintained my twice-a-day meditations. The people who lived in the other houseboats nearby often smoked pot, and the few times I indulged with them cured me of ever wanting to do it again. My roommate financed her education at the Conservatory of Music by playing alto saxophone topless in a North Beach nightclub. One night, a teacher from the Conservatory happened into the nightclub where she was playing, resulting in a quick exchange of embarrassed looks, but for the most part she thought nothing of it.

When we received notice that we would have to leave our houseboat because of a change of ownership, I relocated to a San Francisco one-bedroom apartment, which I shared with a student from San Francisco State College. One morning around 6:00 A.M. my roommate, who was sleeping in the living room, was awakened by a banging on the window. A Christian friend, who lived about four blocks away, sensed something was wrong in our apartment and came by to check things out. The gas wall-heater had malfunctioned causing carbon monoxide poisoning, and we easily could have died. I had a terrible headache and felt so dizzy I could hardly walk that day. Had someone not come by, I might have perished without the mercy and forgiveness of Christ. It was certainly God's intervention in my life.

6

Advanced Training Course

HUMBOLDT COUNTY

I continued to practice TM for several more years before enrolling in an advanced training course to become an instructor. Supposedly, teaching TM would accelerate my evolution toward cosmic consciousness. In order to qualify to attend the teacher-training course, one had to first attend a month-long course of the Science of Creative Intelligence taught by Maharishi. So when August rolled around, I packed up my car and drove north about five hours to Humboldt State College. It was a lovely campus surrounded by redwoods and hills, normally very pristine and quiet. Now the idyllic setting was filled with the bustle of meditators trying to secure their accommodations in the dormitories. The campus gymnasium was transformed into a gigantic assembly hall where we had our nightly meetings.

At this residence course we had to watch the endless video taped lectures by Maharishi held every morning and afternoon. The tapes comprised his entire life teachings and philosophy. As one ex-TM'er put it, "Never has so much been said about so little so brilliantly." The tapes were an appropriate rite of passage into the higher echelons of the TM movement. Finding these tapes boring and monotonous, they often put me to sleep.

When we were not attending Maharishi's taped lectures, we were meditating or eating our meals. Group meditations were held in a large room in the student center during the day, and it was always filled with smoke from burning sandalwood incense. After breathing this incense day in and day out, I became allergic to it and began "serial sneezing" (sometimes 50 or more times), much to the annoyance of other meditators.

Not long after we arrived at the course, those of us unfamiliar with the "asanas" (exercises) were invited to watch a demonstration of them. These were a series of yoga stretching postures that we were to do between meditations. They were supposed to help relieve or prevent a condition called "unstressing," or the discomfort of too much sudden stress release due to the long hours of meditation. I did the asanas faithfully for a long time. They never seemed to do anything for me but hurt my back. Eventually I quit doing them altogether. I was worried that my long neck would finally snap if I kept doing the shoulder stands.

The women in my dormitory daily gathered in the hallways to do the asanas and to chat. Then we would head on down to the meeting hall to hear Maharishi. The dorms were segregated by gender, but one hall mate found a way around it. She always got to lectures late with her boyfriend, their hair wet from taking a shower coeducationally.

It was customary for everyone to wait in a long line to greet Maharishi when he arrived for each session. Many people would go to the store and purchase expensive flowers to hold out to him as he passed by. My friends and I usually picked random scraggly flowers from the roadside. One day I almost succumbed to an urge to offer some dry weeds and thorns to Maharishi, because I could not find any fresh flowers, but I changed my mind at the last minute. This was not due to any disrespect I felt toward Maharishi, but rather to my feeling that the kind of adulation being offered to him was more appropriate for God.

There was a young gay man in the group who always made such an extravagant display of his affection for Maharishi that the yogi would just smile and say, "Love has so many different kinds of expressions." Maharishi sat on a specially covered couch, which was placed on an improvised stage. Some people would run up and bow before him and then be overcome with emotion, which I found to be ridiculous, even disgusting. The entire proceeding was always taped by video cameras.

I remember the first time Maharishi climbed onto his platform and sat down in the lotus posture. We all expected him to start talking, but instead he closed his eyes, and as if on cue, the whole room full of meditators plunged deep into meditation. The energy experienced in group meditation is exponentially greater than when meditating alone. When our group vibes were coupled with the Maharishi's, it was even more intense. These group meditations lasted around 25 minutes. We came out of this meditation by slowly opening our eyes as instructed.

The first several rows in the meeting hall were reserved for the TM teachers and the "higher ups" in the movement. The rest of us plebeians had to sit further back. There were a lot of school teachers at this residence course who were being trained to teach TM in the public schools with the assistance of federal funding. After Maharishi gave his talk, the microphone was open to anyone with questions or comments. I remember being really bored by the many questions Christians would sometimes ask Maharishi, such as: 1) Didn't Christ suffer? 2) How can TM eliminate suffering? 3) What if you see a spirit? 4) Is there any conflict between TM and Christianity?

Someone went up to the microphone and shared that he had some Christian friends at home who claimed to experience the presence of Christ when they prayed. They told him that the presence of the Holy Spirit was there, and that God answered their prayers. He wanted to know what Maharishi thought about that. In response to this question, Maharishi got very agitated, his voice rising in volume and pitch as he adamantly warned that it wasn't Jesus they were encountering, but a demon.

It is reported that during a telephone interview in Brussels (November 30, 1975) Maharishi admitted to a lack of personal relationship with Jesus Christ, when he said:

> How can you feel that Christ is living? It is possible that what is taught contacting Christ is through mediumship. Mediums are highly emotional. Healing in the name of Christ is mediumship. If Jacques invokes Christ, he invokes a spirit. If he is healing in the name of Christ, he has spoiled his life....If our life is in Christ, prayer can become mediumship. It is dangerous to invoke Christ for healing.[5]

During this phone call, Maharishi also said, "*Don't raise the question of Christ before me, because I don't know Him.*" When questioned about how so many Christians seemed to be having spiritual experiences without TM, Maharishi explained that they were just "mood making." These and other issues bored me to sleep when I should have been listening.

One time, right in the middle of the meeting, I heard a man in the back yell, "Liar! Liar!" Totally shocked, everyone turned around to see who was making the commotion, but whoever said it seemed to have a kind of invisible shield around him. After that incident, no one was ever allowed into the room without an I.D. badge. Evidently, a group of Christians who lived in the nearby community had formed an outreach to TM meditators, and most likely they had sneaked into the meeting that night. A group of them were sitting on the lawn the next day as I was passing by. They wanted to know if I would like to come away with them for a visit. This seemed like a very strange invitation since I did not even know them. One of the women in the group just kept smiling at me with a nameless love I did not understand, and I could not look at her. I replied that I couldn't go with them since I was there for teacher training. Some force in me had collided with a stronger force within her, causing me to experience the pull of a spiritual riptide. I was glad to get out of there but puzzled as to how such a minor encounter could ruffle my TM composure.

One day during our free time, a group of us decided to walk down by the stream and to do a little sunbathing "in the natural." At first I was reluctant, but since there were quite a few others, I joined in. While trying to convince myself that this idea arose from our innocent pure consciousness, some non-nude meditators began to gawk at us. I quickly threw my clothes back on and left the scene, hoping no one would remember.

Many of us at the residence course had come out of a semi-hippy lifestyle, and a large number of the men still had long hair or beards. Maharishi didn't like this image because it conflicted with his public relations efforts. Though bearded and scraggly himself, he nevertheless made it clear that all the men were to march up to the barber during the course and submit to the humiliating experience of having themselves shorn. The most radical hairstyle they were allowed to wear was a sort of Beatle haircut. Furthermore, Maharishi stressed the importance of wearing a nice suit and a tie.

Some men grew angry and rebelled at this emphasis on public image, refusing to cut their hair. One complainer came up to the microphone at the question-and-answer period and vented his spleen. I had heard how Maharishi, who never seemed to get mad, could "fry" you with bad vibes if his will was crossed. On this occasion, Maharishi demonstrated his ire, and curtly told everyone that he would not tolerate the long hair. At this point, everyone in the room got a blast of some of the most negative energy I have ever experienced. The men were pale with shock, and many women in the room began to weep. Everyone sat stunned for a long time, and eventually, the meeting was dismissed. The issue was not raised again.

There was one older man at the course who had reportedly passed through cosmic-consciousness and had gone on to God-consciousness. (The official explanation they gave, though I never quite understood it, was that in this state one's heart begins to close the separation between self and activity experienced in cosmic-consciousness.) He was a nice, ordinary looking man perhaps in his early sixties, and I didn't think he seemed especially enlightened or spiritual. He surprised us all one evening by disappearing (or "teleporting") from one side of the room to the other side. There were two microphones, one for each side of the room. First he was at one, then he was at the other, with what seemed like no time lapse in between. We collectively laughed with amazement as we saw this occur. I do not know how he performed this feat, but it seemed to happen naturally without any fanfare. Maybe we were all mesmerized and had gone into a kind of group amnesia, but we all saw it.

It was announced that advanced techniques would be given to those who had been meditating for at least a year and a half. Many of us thought that this technique would be given free of charge, but it cost more than the first technique. I found this to be very unexpected and irritating. After waiting hours beyond the time that Maharishi said he would appear, we had to leave the large room where we had gathered and come back the following day.

Maharishi personally gave us our advanced technique. Half expecting to receive a much more interesting mantra now that I was so "advanced," I was disappointed to find out that it was basically the same mantra, "ing," only with "nama" tacked onto the end: "ing-nama." (I later learned that the meaning of these words in Sanskrit is "Ing," (the Hindu deity's name) "I bow down to you." A couple of years later, I was given yet another advanced technique. It was basically the same mantra, only now "shri" was added, making the translation something like "Oh, most beautiful Ing, I bow down to you." These advanced techniques were supposed to develop the aspect of worship (God-consciousness) even before the advent of cosmic consciousness. Each technique grew longer and more expensive; my first mantra had been $35, the second one $60, and this one was $125. This was a trifling expense compared to what they cost today.

Maharishi's Sidhi program, including Yogic Flying, had not been introduced when I was at the Humboldt course. This program, established in the mid-70s, offered an advanced technique that allegedly enabled meditators to levitate. After only two months of regular practice of TM, meditators could begin the process in bizarre "hopping" sessions. It was supposed to accelerate one's progress toward the state of enlightenment, and it was very expensive. Meditators were promised that indeed they would learn how to fly, but as far as I know, no one has ever done it. As the saying goes, "remove truth, and people will believe almost anything." Nevertheless, Maharishi declared that with the TM-Sidhi program, "we are in a position to create heaven on earth." Such a transformation was, of course, far beyond this guru's power to accomplish.

If you think that "yogic flying" attracts only the outermost fringe, there are at least some celebrities who have become believers. An article from *Newsweek* entitled "Dodging the Yogic Fliers" (July 17, 2000)[6] describes how a quantum physicist named John Hagelin, a TM levitation aspirant and avowed "yogic flier," first entered the Presidential race as the Reform party's opposing candidate to Pat Buchanan. Trained at Harvard, he has worked at prestigious physics labs in Europe and at Stanford University. He made some important discoveries before he got sidetracked by the promise of yogic flying. He found himself "butt hopping" at the Maharishi University of Management in Iowa. Reportedly, he took 4,000 "yogic fliers" to Washington to try to bring down the crime level there through the influence of meditation. In 1999 on the "Roseanne Show," he described sending meditators to Kosovo to stop the violence. Dr. Robert Park, author of the book, *Voodoo Science,* doesn't think he'd feel comfortable, though, with Hagelin running the country.

Early in the course we were invited to learn the checking procedure. With all the meditating and lectures, I found my brain so passive that it was almost impossible to memorize the checking notes, which were extensive. It was here that the mystery of the clone-like quality of the checkers was finally solved. I learned that this whole checking business was really a carefully memorized routine. It was set up something like a computer game or one of those family medical guides in which a "yes" or "no" answer to a question about your symptom channels you into a new series of questions until you finally arrive at the diagnosis. Similarly, every TM complaint was met with a certain series of questions and rote answers resulting inevitably in a monitored meditation session (the ultimate "fix").

7

Mercury and Pluto

WORLDS APART

*M*y departure from the TM program began with my growing dissatisfaction over the lack of integrity I saw in the TM movement. Seeking a revelation of ultimate truth and hungry for a real relationship with God, I eventually began an independent search apart from the confines imposed by the TM lifestyle. I did this in spite of the fact that we had been advised to avoid other spiritual paths. It is surprising that I hadn't reconsidered the claims of Christ, but Christianity was the last place I thought I'd find freedom. As the saying goes, "Been there and done that." Nevertheless, a supernatural chain of events initiated by God set the stage for my exodus from the TM program and led to my total deliverance. What unfolded certainly wasn't something I had planned or even imagined.

Some Campus Crusade for Christ believers provided the catalyst. These dedicated young people set up a table on the Berkeley campus. I thought I could always tell when someone was spiritual by the look in their eyes. These folks had "it"—that mellow look. Their outward demeanor seemed to radiate an inner peace and glow, and so I ventured over to their table and asked them if they practiced TM. I was shocked when they showed me an open Bible and the verse where Jesus said, *"All who ever came before Me are thieves and robbers, but My sheep did not hear them"* (John 10:8). And ... *"I am the way, the truth, and the life. No man can come to the Father except through Me"* (John 14:6).

This divine confrontation cut to the core of my certainty that all paths lead to God. I began to study the Scriptures to see if I could somehow fit TM and Christianity into the same worldview. One book that influenced me at this time was *The Late Great Planet Earth* by Hal Lindsey. He believed that the Bible was entirely true and that humanity was about to enter into the apocalyptic end time prophecies described in the Book of Revelation and the Book of Daniel.

These prophecies foretell a time just before the return of Christ, in which the entire world will be deceived by the Antichrist and the False Prophet and their occult political-religious system. The Bible calls this world government/ world religion "MYSTERY, BABYLON THE GREAT, THE MOTHER OF HARLOTS AND OF THE ABOMINATIONS OF THE EARTH" (Revelation 17:5). Widely tolerated and practiced in this worldview will be various occult practices and beliefs such as astrology, witchcraft, psychic phenomena, meditation, spirit guides, seances, etc. Hal Lindsey pointed out that the Bible calls these evil. Eventually the Antichrist and the False Prophet and all who take the Antichrist's number (represented by the number 666) in the right hand or forehead are defeated and cast into the Lake of Fire, originally reserved for the devil and his fallen angels.

I had a particularly hard time throwing astrology into the same evil bag as the rest, since many of my friends were into astrology, and I just regarded it with a sense of casual disinterest. As for the other practices, I had a "live and let live" attitude. After all, people were in different places in their evolution, and as long as they were not harming anyone, why condemn them?

Hal Lindsey also mentioned a "rapture" experience, where born-again Christians would be "air-lifted" (suddenly disappear) out of the turmoil and trouble of the Tribulation years that precede the return of Christ. (Not all Christians concur on the exact timing of this event.) My first reaction to this was, "Wow! What amazing minds the writers of the Bible must have had! They were probably really evolved." After all, being raptured was probably no more strange than being abducted by a flying saucer or teleporting from one place to another, as in some of the science fiction movies I'd seen. I also began to wonder why people have a hard time believing in the bodily resurrection of Jesus from the dead. Wasn't it just a matter of time before technology would make today's airplane flights (and Jesus' resurrection) seem like yesterday's horse and buggy rides?

At the time I was reading Hal Lindsey's book, I was also reading some prophecies by the psychic Jean Dixon in which she also spoke about a child from the East claiming to be the returned Messiah. She believed that he really would be the Antichrist whose one world political and religious system would deceive the whole world. Although many of her prophecies have proven unreliable, this one at least woke me to the possibility that there even could be such a thing as spiritual deception. Before this, I felt that as long as you were interested in any kind of spiritual things, you'd eventually make it. But good intentions alone have never guaranteed success in any endeavor.

After trying in earnest to fit East and West together, I finally realized that the two would never meet, even though "one world" is the constant mantra of the globally minded. Understandably, most people greatly desire world peace and unity. Christians believe that Jesus is the Messiah and that he came to establish an entirely new creation. The Campus Crusade for Christ witnesses explained that when a person receives Christ, he is changing his citizenship. When Christ returns, He will restore the earth, ruling with His followers (called "saints") for a thousand years of universal peace. After the millennial reign, He will create a new heaven and a new earth.

So according to these believers, while TM belongs to this world and its religious systems, Christianity points to a separate, eternal world. According to their way of thinking, I was trying to reach the spiritual realm of this old dying creation by my own efforts, or passively through meditation. But in the Christianity they were offering me, Christ Himself wanted to pull me from the sinking Titanic of this world system and to join Him in this new creation. They urged me just to respond in faith to His love for me—quite a different thing from trying to create my own salvation through meditation techniques. If what they were saying was true I had a lot of unlearning to do.

At a Campus Crusade Bible study, after a dry, boring, and seemingly uneventful discussion of the Scriptures, one of the people there wanted to know if I had ever asked Jesus into my life. I decided that the group needed a little livening up, so I fabricated a story that I had heard Jesus knocking on the door to my house. I told them that after inviting Him in, I saw Him walk into my living room. No one in the Bible study was visibly convinced (or impressed.) They were very polite and listened quietly, but one fellow sitting in the back just shook his head sadly.

In my fabrication of this Jesus encounter, I was following a principle I had learned from some of the New Age groups I had visited. Some groups teach that they can use the power of what they say to influence or create their own destiny. What difference, then, if they "edit" the story line of their past life history a little? This would not be considered lying, but simply refashioning their identity in order to achieve a better future. But is truth really negotiable?

When I finally became aware that any attempt to join my TM path with Christianity would be ultimately and eternally impossible, I put Jesus on the shelf and opted to continue what I seemed to know best. And that was to continue TM. In fact, I was now determined to go ahead with Phase II of my plans for becoming a TM teacher.

8

Becoming a TM Instructor

FIUGGI, ITALY

*M*ore than 2,000 meditators from all over the world gathered in Fiuggi, Italy, for three months of personal and group instruction under Maharishi. This included six weeks of intensive meditation and six weeks of instruction. Being with the guru himself was supposed to impart a special power, and becoming a TM teacher was guaranteed to speed up one's evolution toward cosmic-consciousness.

When we first arrived at the teacher-training course in Fiuggi, there was the usual scramble to try to find the hotel or house where we would be staying. Since many TM teachers paid their way for the residence courses by being cooks, you either had a great meal experience or you half starved, depending on which cook you had. Quality control was clearly lacking because some of my friends groaned about the "thin watery vegetable stews with hardly anything else in them." Being thin to start with, I was grateful that we had delicious vegetarian meals with lots of variety at our house.

When one undergoes a teacher-training course that involves long and extensive meditations, things can get pretty weird for the meditator. But anything out of the ordinary is usually explained away as "unstressing." All of my unstressing seemed to hit me at meal times when I became withdrawn and paranoid. Trying to hide these low-level feelings only compounded my stress. Things sometimes built up to such a point that I could only get relief by soaking away my tensions in a bath mixed with relaxing essential oils such as ylang-ylang or lavender.

At this course we meditated for as much as 8-12 hours a day, interspersed with yoga stretching exercises ("asanas"). We also did "pranayama" breathing exercises by alternatingly closing off one nostril at a time (supposedly to calm the mind and prepare one for meditation). Maharishi told us that either asanas or pranayamas alone were powerful enough to slowly bring one to cosmic-consciousness. Alternating them with meditation was called "rounding." Some people rounded 16 to 20 hours a day. I saw one such person leaning against the wall, eyes vacant—"nobody home."

One really nice guy that I met at the course started exhibiting extreme personality changes. He would walk to the meadow and sit for hours staring at the ants or other insects. Then he would come back and tell me about it, all in great detail. One of my friends there was genuinely depressed, but she couldn't get counseling from anyone. Repeatedly she was told that she was just unstressing and that she needed to shorten her meditation times for a while. This really hurt her feelings and made her even more despondent. Occasionally someone would break out in sores as a result of unstressing, then heal "properly." TMers believe that there are many different kinds of "unresolved" stresses (such as incomplete resolution of illness in the body) that TM brings to a head and then finally resolves completely. But I had my doubts. Sometimes I felt like I was in a nuthouse. These and many other stories about the various kinds of unstressing could fill a book.

LACK OF INTEGRITY

Being a TM teacher enlarged and clarified my view of the entire movement and highlighted the lack of integrity I was already beginning to suspect. Because I had asked Jesus into my life when I was a child, the Spirit of Truth (another name for God) began faithfully to deliver me out of deception by causing me to become really disgusted by the inconsistencies and lying evident in the TM movement.

For instance, in preparing to become teachers of TM, we knew that it was not merely a neutral, scientific technique for gaining deep rest and other benefits. Plainly put, a person who practiced TM was engaging in a form of Hindu religious practice, whether he or she realized it or not. We were told, however, to present TM to the public as merely a scientific exercise because they were not evolved enough to understand the spiritual transformation they would be experiencing. Maharishi explained the reason for this split-level reality of TM in his commentary on the Bhagavad-Gita:

> If the enlightened man wants to bless one who is ignorant, he should...try to lift him up from there by giving him the key to transcending (i.e., TM), so that he may gain bliss-consciousness and experience the Reality of Life. He should not tell him about the level of the realized because it would only confuse him.[7]

Personally, I felt like a hypocrite and a liar every time I presented TM to the public in this manner. Moreover, I began to experience a devastating spiritual emptiness as a result of TM, a coldness that seemed to be devoid of real love. Although it seemed that TM had given me some of the promised benefits, such as better health, confidence and a measure of success, it also opened me a dark realm of lawless spirits and psychic phenomena. The lack of love in the meditators (and also in myself) served as a warning to my conscience that something very essential was missing.

During one of the regular group meetings with Maharishi at the Fiuggi teacher-training course, this lack of love became obvious. One of the meditators sitting right behind me fell off a chair into what seemed like a comatose state from over-meditating. Yet no one tried to help her or even seemed to care. Eventually, some people came and carried her off. I was too stoned from all my many hours of meditating to understand or feel any compassion for her, but one man nearby was visibly disgusted by the lack of caring.

"JUST INVITE THEM IN"

Then there was the problem of demonic manifestations. Nobody likes to talk about that. Meditation has been described as a deep passivity combined with awareness. But at times, there is a phenomenon called the "blackout." I used to go blank for ten minutes or longer (sometimes up to an hour) during my meditations and not remember anything that went on during that time. I was fortunate to be able to resist being possessed, but others were not so protected, and some wound up in psych wards. There was a general lack of awareness or concern on the part of TM meditators to these situations.

Maharishi had told us to resist a demon if it tried to "bother" us, but on another occasion, I heard him say, "Don't be afraid, *just invite them in.*" Maharishi did not acknowledge the reality of good and evil. He said that everything is merely an extension of our minds. This mentality led to a dangerous kind of openness that made demonic possession or oppression all the more possible. When a powerful demon tried to possess me one night while

I was sleeping, I had only a few semi-conscious seconds to decide which advice to take: (resist or invite). Because my early Christian upbringing had taught me to resist evil, I rejected the advances of this spiritual entity and did not invite it in. But the experience was very scary.

After memorizing the entire *Puja*—no easy task with minds like Swiss cheese from all the meditating—we had to prove our knowledge by taking an oral exam. Just ahead of me in line was an older German lady, weeping and distraught because she could not remember all of the words of the *Puja*. She flunked the test after only a few attempts and was disqualified from being a TM teacher. I felt really sorry for her.

The climactic event when becoming a teacher of TM was going through a grand initiation held in the basement of a large building and presided over by Maharishi. Going down the steps and entering the huge room filled with the smoke of incense and lined with candlelit *Puja* tables all around was like walking into a strange subterranean cavern. I found it eerie and a little frightening. At one end of the room, Maharishi was sitting on his special throne-like platform.

One began by performing a *Puja* at the nearest table and then continuing on through many *Pujas* until reaching Maharishi. The *Puja* has a powerful effect upon the consciousness. TM teachers often said that they saw visions of Guru Dev, Maharishi's departed master, or other spirits while performing the *Puja*. By the time I finished, I was so dizzy and disoriented I hardly knew what I was doing. During this initiation of teachers, we received the list of the mantras, dictated to us in a special room through the use of earphones. We were told to keep the mantras secret, and to my surprise, I discovered that the mantras were given out only on the basis of one's age, not on one's spiritual level or any other factor. When the course was over, I returned to the Berkeley area to live and taught at the Students' International Meditation Center (SIMS) for about a year until something happened that was to radically change the course of my life forever.

FLYING SAUCER CULT
Uninvited Visitors

After returning from Italy, there was an adjustment period of several weeks during which we gradually shortened the duration and frequency of our meditation times. Everything started looking strangely real again. At first, everyone seemed to be moving and talking too fast because I was thinking and moving so slowly. Now that I was a TM teacher, it was gratifying to my ego to be regarded with a kind of awe by the others, and there was a great "in-group" feeling among us teachers. Many of us felt that the initiations would have a powerful effect on our own consciousness. After one particular initiation, I felt so high and dizzy, I had to lie down on the floor afterwards.

First graduating class (Vail is on far right)

There was a man who physically could not bend his knees before the altar of Guru Dev. He received this as a warning from God and since that time dropped the practice of TM altogether and went into full-time Christian ministry. We heard about a Jewish girl who literally ran out of the _Puja_ room, convicted that the bowing down before the altar of Guru Dev was blatant idolatry forbidden by the Scriptures.

I began to eat vegetarian meals at the One World Family Restaurant, conveniently located just a few blocks from my apartment in Berkeley. It was run by a flying saucer cult, which served up outstanding vegetarian fare. Most of the clientele were New Age devotees, of course, but one couple—an older man and his much younger wife—who came in regularly for supper, seemed to stand out. They had a peace and a unity about them that fascinated me.

I tried to recruit one of their close friends who worked behind the serving line, telling him how high TM can make you feel, but I wasn't expecting the response I got. His views undoubtedly had been influenced by that Christian couple I had often seen at the restaurant. He responded, "I don't think that TM is very high at all," adding that he was turned off by forms of meditation that have no real "fruit" and don't result in real improvement in peoples' lives. That was the first time I had run into anyone who had openly doubted the value of TM. This new twist gave me much to ponder.

It was commonly known that the owner of the restaurant, Allan Noonan, regularly channeled spirits or "aliens" during his trances in the back of the restaurant. He wrote an alternative version of the standard teachings of the Bible based on these encounters. Every evening after I had finished eating, I would go to the back of the restaurant where he had been channeling and meditate for my evening TM session. Many times a spirit sat beside me. Once, I turned and saw it. This one was a voracious looking little demon with sharp teeth, not the beautiful angel I expected. But since it made no aggressive movements toward me, I did not think it was dangerous.

When one of my TM friends, a nice young Jewish girl named Lennie, decided to spend the night at their commune located near the restaurant, she had a vision of what appeared to be an "invasion" of strange evil looking creatures coming in through the closed window. These creatures seemed to fit the description of the one that sat with me as I meditated in the restaurant. I knew that meditators can sometimes have bizarre supernatural visions and experiences, but this one really shook Lennie up. Somehow, the official TM explanation that she was going through "unstressing" just didn't seem to fit. From that point on, she had deep misgivings about the New Age movement and TM in particular, and so did I.

Occasionally at night, spirits would come and quietly sit on my bed. I was not dreaming; these experiences were very real. The bed even seemed to physically move. Maharishi had told us not to focus on the spirits, but to keep our mind on the goal of enlightenment. However, I couldn't help wondering what they were up to.

NEARLY PERFECT LIFE

Shortly afterward, I decided to move into a large residence for TM teachers located in the north part of Berkeley. Life there in many ways seemed ideal. I was a young, 29-year-old with lots of friends (mostly other TM teachers). I enjoyed my freelance artwork, my job at the TM meditation center, and occasional weekend retreats. When I wasn't attending TM meetings or checking meditations, I pursued a fashion-modeling career on the side. To compensate for feelings of a poor body image from skinny adolescent days and occasional classmate teasing ("pale Vail, skinny as a rail"), I decided that I would turn my leanness into an asset. But even though I completed modeling school and was in a few fashion shows, I failed to produce a completed portfolio of snapshots. Although some said I had the height and the "look," I finally agreed with my mother's observation that modeling can be a vain "dog-eat-dog" world. This career never really materialized.

Vail modeling

Everything in my life seemed nearly perfect, but something was missing and others must have felt it, too. The lovely stucco house where we lived accommodated at least fifteen meditators. One evening, we heard a scream and hysterical shouting. A woman who had been at the same teacher-training course that I had attended was demanding to know where the scissors were so she could kill herself. Several people in the house tried to calm her down, but she screamed and cried for a long time. They assured her that she was just "unstressing," and that she would be over it soon. Moreover, several married TM teachers were getting divorced at this time. Obviously, not everyone was experiencing the promised bliss.

One day while standing around and visiting in the front office of the TM center, I overheard someone say that one of the TM teachers had "defected" and joined up with a group of born-again Christians. I was stunned by this and could not understand how someone that far advanced in TM could stop meditating and go back to *just* being a Christian. I took a closer look at the woman who had said this. She was one of the more level-headed, "real" people there, not spaced out like some of the rest.

She gave a longing look tinged with a touch of envy and said, "I have seen these Christians, and probably the reason she joined them is that they have so much love, real love for one another." Years later, I was to read in the Scriptures where Jesus said, *"By this all men will know that you are My disciples, if you have love for one another"* (John 13:35). I guess when you get down to what I was really looking for it was love, sweet love. I had been raised in a loving home, but I needed to experience God's love. And that love was impossible to find in TM.

Like so many people in today's society, I was

desperate for meaningful answers. Maharishi had advised against going to a psychic, but I was impatient to know when I would be entering cosmic consciousness. A friend of mine and I went to one, hoping she would be able to give us some information. At the beginning of my session with her, I had a curiously sickening feeling as she went into a deep trance and began to speak into a tape recorder. For about half an hour she told me a lot of things about my family and upbringing, most of it way off base. Only after the "change" in my spiritual path did I realize that consulting psychics can easily lead a person astray. You can be deceived because some things the psychics tell you are partially true. For instance, she said I would be changing my spiritual path and that my new friends would be "of a very different energy" from my current TM associations. Also, she said that if I were to meet these people now, I would not appreciate them. In that, she was probably right.

9

No Other Name Under Heaven

A UNIQUE APPROACH

*W*hile many people's lives have been transformed through the plain presentation of the Bible, God chose a nontraditional approach with me. He had to reach way around my discarded childhood religion and reveal Himself in a different way. He chose to use a yogi named Sean, a psychic who had dabbled in many different spiritual paths, including Christianity. I had seen him on campus one day and recognized something in him that seemed to set him apart from the crowd. Even though, as Sean later admitted, he had not yet made a breakthrough to knowing the Lord, God had used him to bring salvation to many others. He promoted a unique approach he termed "calling on the name of the Lord." I want to make it clear that I had come to a point in my life where I was willing to do almost anything to find God. I was willing to lay down all my preconceptions, all my hopes and desires, with only one burning desire, to KNOW HIM!

Sean held a series of classes in which a group of us joined hands and tuned into various psychic or spiritual fields or beings, including Buddha, Mohammed, and other famous spiritual leaders. He also told us to call on the name of a friend. Finally, we were told to call on the name of

Jesus, the "Name above all names." Sean explained that this would deliver us out of the bondage of this created world into the realm of the Creator himself. He said that this would be like the relationship a child would experience with its mother or father, and that we were to call out to Jesus as a child would to a loving parent. This much Sean got right.

For about a week, I continued to call upon the name of the Lord Jesus Christ in addition to my silent TM meditation. It was initially very difficult to call upon that name. It seemed to get stuck somewhere in my larynx. Sean said that there was power in the spoken word, unlike the TM technique, which conceals the hidden mantra. So out loud, I called to Jesus to save, touch, and deliver me. I also asked Him to cleanse me. "All the other ways will make you blissful; this name, Jesus will make you *clean*," Sean said. That was a new concept for me. For years, I had been trying to get high, when what I really needed was to be spiritually cleansed. Then I could have the good feelings I was searching for. The relational aspect of calling out to God as a personal Being also was new to me.

But the more I called upon His name, the smaller and punier I began to feel. My ego was getting crushed. No one had ever told me that you could lose your expanded state of consciousness! I thought that the name of Jesus must be very powerful if it could do that. Nothing seemed to take Sean by surprise. He explained that the name of Jesus is so purifying that it starts to purge all the impurities we carry around inside us. "It's the church upbringing you had that makes you feel so bad about Christianity," he said. Actually, my church upbringing really wasn't a big issue with me. "Just continue calling on the name of Jesus, and you'll get beyond all that."

Though my foundations were shaking, I continued to press through because I felt that eventually I would be free. However, I almost quit right before the breakthrough.

A BLUE GOD
Or Cosmic Soup

While revisiting the Hare Krishna group on the Berkeley campus, I was warned by their leader (a very devoted and honest man) that TM was a deception. He said that in TM we were being taught that God is already in us, but they worshipped Krishna who they said is separate from them. There may be variations in what different Krishna groups believe, but that is what they taught. To illustrate his point, he presented an analogy: "Picture a green tree with a green bird on one of its branches," he said. "The bird does not become the tree but remains a bird." This really appealed to me because I had always felt uncomfortable with the impersonal view of God presented by TM.

An important part of the advanced teaching behind TM was the idea that at the end of one's spiritual journey through many incarnations, one reaches a state of enlightenment. Eventually one dissolves into an infinite Ocean of Being. All personal characteristics cease, similar to what happens when a drop of water falls into the sea. This is referred to as "merging with the Godhead."

I had two problems with this concept. First, it was scary. Who wants to lose their identity and merely return to a huge cosmic soup? I was never too happy when they started talking about that. It seemed like spiritual suicide. Second, I instinctively recognized a severe ego problem with the idea that *we* are *it*. Being a worshipper and a servant of God seemed better than wanting to BE God. The Krishna devotees were right on that point. Certainly the belief system their leader described to me seemed closer to the Christian concept of humanity being the *image* of God rather than part of His essence. However, I had a hard time relating to Krishna, the little blue man with a flute. My mom and my dad weren't blue. I'm not blue. And I really hoped that God wasn't blue.

While with this group, I enjoyed listening to their chanting and dancing, so I began to dance along with them. For the first time, I experienced an overwhelming love for God who knew I was truly seeking Him. My dancing was really an expression of this pure worship that I felt for Him (not Krishna). Afterward, we joined their leader, Robbie, as he sat down on the lawn in his long, colorful robe. He opened a large book and began to read from one of their Hindu texts, *The Bhagavad Gita.* I had previously developed a friendship with Robbie, and he and some of his devoted associates had visited me at my apartment. His whole life was devoted to Krishna, his every thought was focused on him, and he continually gave praise to Krishna. I found that to be unique and somehow endearing because I had not seen that kind of total life dedication in my experience of Christianity. Once-a-week, lukewarm, Sunday morning services and then "life as usual" seemed totally "underwhelming." No one told me that you could live a relevant life wholly abandoned to the Lord without being a monk or a nun.

While we listened to Robbie read, he suddenly stopped and looked intently at me. He told me, "You are going to find God because you are sincere." Something started breaking free inside my spirit because his voice was like a spiritual megaphone through which I heard divine words spoken. Sometimes we try to put God in a box and think he can only speak to us certain ways. But God chooses when and in what way He will speak to us, even if He has to break us out of our usual patterns. After this, Robbie began to read these words from the text: _"God has three infinite aspects: Knowledge, Power, and Bliss."_

A BURNING SENSE

There was a burning sense in my heart that something of monumental importance was about to happen. Before returning to my apartment, I was standing outside the Student Union talking with some friends. As I looked across at some trees, I noticed with awe that they appeared to be somehow clapping their hands in the wind. I had to blink my eyes and do a reality check. Sure enough, the trees seemed to be praising God. I was unaware of the Bible verse that says, _"For you shall go out with joy, and be led out with peace; the mountains and the hills shall break forth into singing before you. And all the trees of the field shall clap their hands"_ (Isaiah 55:12). Back in my apartment, I pulled out a book from my bookshelf. As I randomly flipped through the pages, it fell open to a passage which read, _"God has three infinite aspects: Knowledge, Power, and Bliss."_ I was totally stunned.

In the light of such an unusual day, it seemed fitting that I should pray, something I had not done in a long time. That night, I decided to recite the Lord's Prayer. Just saying the Lord's Prayer would have been a major development in my life, if nothing else. When I got to the words, _"For Thine is the Kingdom, the Power, and the Glory,"_ suddenly there was a powerful burst of brilliant white light. Immediately I remembered the words, _"Knowledge, Power, and Bliss."_ Undoubtedly, God was up to something, and my spiritual throttle was at full tilt!

GALLERY OF THE GURUS

The following night, I decided to make things simpler by taking down all the pictures of spiritual masters and gurus that I had put on the wall: Maharishi and his departed master Guru Dev, Krishna, Buddha, Yogananda, and all other pictures except for one, Jesus Christ. I hung this picture about six feet from my bed. The room after that felt much brighter and cleaner. Just as I went to bed, I heard a knock at the door. It was Sean. He asked me if I wanted to come into the living room to call on the name of Jesus with him as we had done many times before. I was sleepy, but I managed to crawl out of bed.

We had only been calling on His name a few minutes when something unexpected happened. The heavenly light of God's inimitable presence and glory filled the room. I felt connected and alive, like a small child full of wonder and awe. As this was occurring, cords of bondage previously unknown to me were being released. I do not know how long I was in this state because I lost all sense of time and felt weightless. The purest love imaginable emanating from the heart of God poured through every part of my being, wave upon wave. Sean noticed it and said, "I saw you go 'up,' but I did not go myself," whereupon he looked strangely afraid.

When I went into my bedroom, the picture of Jesus that had been on the wall was now right beside my pillow. (See picture insert.) Upon seeing that, I had a vision of something like a flaming arrow piercing my heart with an indescribable love that would change me forever. I broke and began to cry. I realized that God was revealing a new kind of love to me—unconditional, permanent and totally undeserved. By placing the picture right near my pillow, He was sending an undeniable message that He is a Friend who will always "stick closer than a brother" (Proverbs 18:24). The realization that God was tangibly real and loved me was almost more than I could contain.

In that very instant I was healed from the hurt caused by the deaths of my father and stepfather, from disappointing relationships, rejections, and many fears. My dignity as a human being was restored. I felt like God's rightful child, and I knew that I had a secure relationship with Him that nothing could take away.

That night God gave me a breathtaking dream. In this dream I was taking a bath in the living room in a beautiful, porcelain white bathtub unattached to any wall. Water was pouring out of the faucet and filling up the tub where I was bathing. When I pulled out the plug, the water drained out over the rug in blood. While the thought of blood is repellent to most people, this blood was no ordinary blood—it was holy, pure, and full of life-changing power. We have to see spiritual truths with born-again vision. By this, the Lord showed me that I had been "washed in His blood" and baptized in the Holy Spirit by His grace. In the dream Sean was also taking a bath, but it was in the bathroom in a *man-made* tub attached to a *natural* water source. In spite of his psychic abilities, he was not washed in the blood of the Lamb or baptized in the Holy Spirit. That part of the dream revealed to me that Sean had not yet fully trusted Christ.

In spite of the magnificence of my conversion experience, I feel that the most essential life-changing event—the real miracle—occurred when I finally surrendered to Christ. Though the outward event occurred in the room with Sean, the real event took place in the privacy of my own heart without any sales pitch or fanfare, and before any signs or wonders. God first wooed my heart then won me.

Picture of Jesus that relocated

GOD'S PRESENCE
Jesus Freak at Last

The next day, I was so filled with joy, I ran down the street singing the "Hallelujah Chorus," and I sensed the rejoicing of angels. As I ran, I looked up into the sky and saw that even the clouds were being moved by the invisible, awesome hand of God. You cannot imagine the freedom and happiness I was experiencing. Everywhere I went, I told people what had happened and how I had found God. Right after my conversion, some people told me that they could feel God's powerful presence emanating from me. To others, however, I was now just another "Jesus freak." With my background I really enjoyed presenting the true Jesus to New Agers and meditators because I had "been there" and knew all their alibis. At a restaurant one day someone told me that they thought I was "the most articulate Jesus freak" they had ever met. But my happiness no longer depended on the approval of other people, and that was a huge change for me. I enjoyed the feeling of safety and protection in this eternal realm of the Creator, something I never had in the psychic realm of TM.

After finding Jesus, there was a period of about six months before I was able to fully comprehend all the ramifications of the wonderful new life I had been given. Right away, I experienced what it meant to be a new creation. *"Therefore, if anyone is in Christ, he is a new creation; old things have passed away; behold, all things have become new"* (2 Corinthians 5:17). One day I told a group of Christians visiting in my apartment that I felt like I was being carried in the arms of a flowing river. I had never experienced such peace before, or such joy. These Christians said that at first God carries us like a baby. Then we have to grow up and walk on our own, and that the "river feeling" would soon pass.

I know now that the river is the River of God that is sweeping many into revival in these last days. God is calling us to enter that stream, to come into the fullness of His Life. Although I agree that we have to grow into maturity,

I don't think we need to lose our experience of the River. Sometimes a babe in Christ knows things the older ones should not have forgotten. The Scriptures tell us that absolutely nothing can separate us from God's love. *"Who shall separate us from the love of Christ? Shall tribulation, or distress, or persecution, or famine, or nakedness, or peril, or sword?"* (Romans 8:35).

God will even use our blunders, in spite of ourselves, and cover us with His tender mercies during our infant Christian beginnings. Shortly after I was saved, I took a bus called the "Grey Tortoise" from San Francisco to New York City to attend my brother's wedding. It was an experience I don't think I'll ever forget. There were about thirty of us on board, and it took four days to get there. We slept sardine style on wall-to-wall rubber mats except for the six hanging navy bunks. During the day we sat on the mats or in one of the three rows of regular bus seats in the front. Some of the travelers were pot smokers, so like it or not, I had to breathe the same air a good part of the time. I just prayed and asked Jesus to cover and protect me. I did not experience one physical discomfort usually associated with long trips. We stopped frequently, bathed in streams and hot springs, and ate picnics at choice locations along the way. One of the places we visited was the Indiana sand dunes by Lake Michigan, the most beautiful lake I've ever seen. We swam in a stream in Omaha, Nebraska, in the rain, and afterward the bus driver decided that the best way for him to dry off was to drive naked for a while. Once while we were having a picnic at a beautiful spot in the country, one of the girls traveling with us decided to totally disrobe. She stood eating her sandwich stark naked while all the guys tried to act cool, but I knew it was totally wrong. The hippies seemed to place a high status on public nudity for some reason.

I witnessed to about half of the members of the bus trip, although it would have been much better if I had traveled with Christians. At one of our stops, I noticed a girl sitting on the ground spreading out her tarot cards. She was a former "Jesus freak" who had gotten sidetracked into astrology among other things. I told her how Jesus wanted to provide her with true guidance and wisdom and that she could really know the Lord. Showing a change of heart, she put her cards away and began to ask me a lot of questions about God. By the end of the trip, I was pretty sure she had turned her life completely over to Christ.

The bus broke down once and ran out of gas, and it also blew a tire in New York City because there are so many broken bottles on the street. A friend of the bus driver invited us to spend the night at his apartment, but a few of us stayed behind in the bus. One girl who had told me she was traveling to marry her fiancé returned the next morning arm in arm with her new lover, the bus driver. I felt sorry for her fiancé.

When it came time to return to the West Coast, I took the "Grey Rabbit," similar to the other bus but furnished differently. The whole inside was nothing but individual bunks stacked two or three high. It was interesting from a sociological viewpoint how the first bus fostered friendships and better witnessing. This one made us more isolated and wasn't much fun either.

When I got home, my happiness in being a Christian was so compelling that I called the psychic I had visited to tell her that I had found God. It really shook her up when I told her that God loves me just the way I am and that He had given me complete spiritual fulfillment and joy right "where I was at" without reaching the TM goal of cosmic consciousness.

It was impossible to avoid evoking a negative reaction from some just because "the good news" wasn't always what people wanted to hear. At this time I went through many spiritual battles in which I encountered some demons that had been deceiving me for a long time. When I was in TM, many of them had disguised themselves as spirits or angels. Now some would come at me during the night and try to choke, paralyze, or generally harass me; but every time I called upon the name of Jesus or the Blood of Jesus, the demons had to leave immediately.

TOSSING OLD RELICS

One of the first things I did after I discovered the reality of Jesus Christ (as well as the reality of Satan) was to throw out or burn old relics from my former life that had anything whatsoever to do with the occult or Eastern mysticism. Although this was not something I was counseled to do, my old TM and occult stuff seemed to exude the sickening sweet smell of "ant poison." I don't know how to describe it any better. You know it's sweet, but you know it will kill you just the same! Looking at it gave me a terrible feeling in my heart. Even now, when I walk into a store where they sell occult items, I still smell ant bait and have that sickening feeling.

Some things I hated to get rid of because of great sentimental or monetary value, so I decided that I would be extravagant in my love for Jesus and throw them away. I even got rid of a valuable Egyptian lapis and gold scarab ring that had an occult meaning. My friends and I made a huge bonfire. Into it went all of my diaries (I sometimes regret being *that* extreme), much of my artwork, and many books, magazines, and various paraphernalia that opposed the true message of salvation and did not glorify the Savior.

I wanted to destroy any remnants of things that had occult "roots." Later I noticed that others who had failed to do this experienced years of subtle oppression, or even outright attacks upon them or their family, such as sickness, accidents, strife, and divorce, or rebellion in their children. Satan derives pleasure from destroying lives. I did a thorough housecleaning and asked the Lord to show me if there were any objects in my home that give demonic beings legal ground "to stand on." Jesus said that He is the "narrow gate." Though that gate may at times seem "strait" (confining), through Him one can find freedom, not enslavement. *"I am the door. If anyone enters by Me, he will be saved, and will go in and out and find pasture"* (John 10:9).

Much later in my Christian life I learned something else you can do to clear your dwelling of any remaining interference, and that is to anoint your home with oil—windows, doorways, etc. When we pray and anoint our homes in the name of the Father, Son, and Holy Spirit, the demons must flee. They will see the anointing oil as the blood of Christ like they did in the days when the Israelites placed the blood of a lamb over their doorways. The destroying angel passed over and did them no harm. You may use a special anointing oil, but any oil will do. If you are desperate, you can get out some Crisco or motor oil. There is no inherent "magic" to the oil; it is only a tangible symbol of the Holy Spirit. When used with faith in conjunction with the Name of Jesus, demons have to go. When you have sent them all out, you may seal the last door with the oil. Once in a while, you may want to do a "house cleansing" touch-up if you or your family members have been facing any particular spiritual oppression (which can happen to any of us at times).

SALVATION "ANANDA"
Salvation Bliss

I attended only one more TM meeting. The Lord comforted and encouraged me during the meeting by literally and unexpectedly holding my right hand until I was out of the meditation center and on my way home. I could not see the Lord, but I knew that it was His hand. Although this experience seemed amazing to me, I later discovered a scripture that substantiated my experience. It is found in Isaiah 41:13: *"For I, the Lord your God, will hold your right hand, saying to you, 'Fear not, I will help you.'"* The Holy Spirit, that great guiding Friend, advised me not to return to my old TM friends, but to let them come to me. As if on cue, all of my regular friends stopped calling me. But after my salvation, a couple of TM teachers, having heard of my conversion, came over to my apartment and tried to convince me that because of the many spiritual experiences I was having, I had entered into cosmic consciousness and also perhaps a bit of God-consciousness as well.

Although this sounded appealing, I rejected it because I KNEW that I had personally met Christ and that only His costly sacrifice and amazing love had given me this wonderful new life. It wasn't Transcendental Meditation or the level of my awareness that had brought about this transformation. It had been given freely to me by God and received through faith, but not blind faith. My experience of salvation was the real bliss or happiness ("ananda") that the new spiritualities could not deliver. And this precious gift cost God everything!

If this sounds naive and too simplistic, could it be because there is no ego satisfaction in being "saved?" TM meditators consider attaining cosmic consciousness a great achievement, and that secretly appeals to their pride. But I knew in my heart that Jesus' love had purchased this priceless gift of everlasting life for me on the cross. I dared not attribute salvation to anything I had done, lest through pride I become disqualified to receive it. So I rejected the temptation to attribute my joy to anything other than the simple reality of finding and knowing Him.

Although the TM organization tried to keep it "hush-hush," quite a few TM initiators also found Jesus around the time that I did. Former TM teachers Toni and Renee Brazil wrote SCP (the Berkeley-based Spiritual Counterfeits Project that studies and researches many cults). They described a phone call by Maharishi to twenty-five Belgian TM teachers who had gathered from the entire country. Although not Belgian, this couple was present at the meeting where they were able to take notes as he spoke. Evidently a crisis had arisen within the Belgian TM movement—similar to a factory suffering a strike by half its workers. Some Belgian initiators had sensed a conflict between TM and their own Catholic Christian faith. One of Maharishi's closest teachers, Jacques, was "the boy" of Maharishi for about one year before leaving him. He had enjoyed the revered, traditional, Master-disciple relationship. He had the most honored position possible in the organization: personal valet, chauffeur, food bearer, security guard, etc.

Jacques was called by the Lord Jesus from a very young age. He was quite intelligent and had a Ph.D. in chemistry. He had been very important in the TM movement and was responsible for the national Belgian TM organization. Because Jacques allowed the Lord Jesus to use his testimony, half of the Belgian initiators (twelve) stopped meditating and returned to the Catholic faith. Maharishi was very angry during this phone call, and the air evidently was "hot." He said that they "needed more rest," were "abusing the knowledge," and other false arguments. No other group provoked Maharishi's anger more than the Christians who hold fast to the cross as their only salvation because this is in complete contradiction to his teachings. After this phone conversation some went back to meditating and teaching, but others continued in fidelity to the Gospel. Tony and Renee Brazil were among the latter group.

MY BACK PROBLEM
Proof of Healing

The many hours of required meditation at the residence courses had caused me a lot of back pain that never went away, but rather grew worse. In an attempt to stabilize my condition, I wore a pair of therapeutic shoes. Nothing seemed to stop the pain, which was gradually increasing in severity. My chiropractor, Frank Young (who had been named "Chiropractor of the Year") diagnosed me as having a degenerating condition of the spine. This was not the last word, however. While spending the night at my mother's house and having difficulty sleeping because of the back pain, I placed my hand on my back and asked Jesus to please heal me, adding that I knew He still healed today. Suddenly, it was as if someone had taken a big dipper and poured invisible, tingly, gold dust all over me from the top of my head to the bottom of my feet. It was His glory! Along with this experience and the heavenly joy that accompanied it, the pain left for good. I felt that I had been given a brand new spine.

I was eager to document the healing, so I asked my chiropractor to take new x-rays of my spine and to write a letter verifying the healing. His evaluation of the "before and after" x-rays is as follows:

It was not anticipated that the curvature would improve significantly. Our main interest was to correct the misaligned vertebra to rid her of the pinched nerve causing her sciatica. A re-examination was performed on Ms. Vail approximately two years later showing a remarkable change in her spine. Her right leg now was the same length as her left leg; the idiopathic scoliosis (spinal curve) was eliminated; and the spine had taken on a complete new appearance. Upon questioning Ms. Vail about this remarkable change, she told me the story of her experience with Christ. There is no scientific explanation for what happened. However, due to the nature and the extent of the change, I feel that there was some outside influence. I accept her explanation.[8] [See photos, next page.]

I showed these photos to my mother but she assumed that the spinal condition probably was corrected through physical exercise. After I showed her Dr. Young's letter, however, she was not so sure. Spiritual healings happen frequently, but it is rare to have documented proof. There is so much more to Christianity than you will find in some churches. As Tommy Tenney wrote in his book *The God Chasers,*

Once you experience God in His glory, you can't turn away from Him or forget His touch. It's not just an argument or a doctrine; it's an experience. That is why the apostle Paul said, *"...I know whom I have believed..."* (2 Tim.1:12). Unfortunately, many people in the Church would say, "I know about whom I have believed." That means they haven't met Him in His glory.[9]

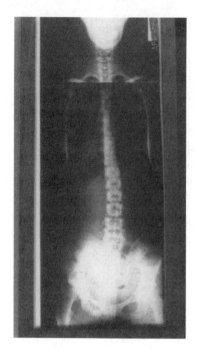 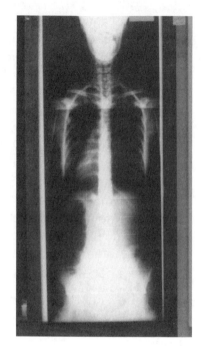

Before and after x-rays of spine healing

10

Light or Darkness?

KNOWING THE DIFFERENCE

*A*lthough my TM friends no longer called me or came over, it was very satisfying to tell them about my experience with Christ whenever the opportunity arose. I was strengthened by a vision the Lord gave me about Berkeley. The Lord showed me that He is going to take this city that has a worldwide reputation for being a place of unrest, rebellion, cynicism, and intellectual pride, and resurrect it from spiritual death.

During my TM days, I formed a relationship with a charming couple, a tall beauty from Denmark and a successful American businessman. They were probably my closest friends. One day after my conversion while I was in one of the many Berkeley bookstores, I ran into Peter and told him about my experience with Christ and that I no longer practiced TM. He gave me an incredulous look. I showed him a scripture that I felt would prove to him that Jesus wasn't just a "force" or state of consciousness, but a real living Being. *"But I make known to you, brethren, that the gospel which was preached by me is not according to man. For I neither received it from man, nor was I taught it, but it came through the revelation of Jesus Christ"* (Galatians 1:11-12). No flicker of light or recognition crossed his face. I think he felt I had gone "nuts" and was now parroting gibberish. Not knowing what else to do, I prayed for him after I left the bookstore. I remembered reading in the Bible that we should endeavor to sow the Word wherever we can and leave the results up to God, who will bring someone else along to water that seed.

I had another chance to be a witness to one of my TM friends at the laundromat. This time I think that I had more noticeable success. After sharing with her about why I had left TM, I showed her this scripture: *"For it is written, I will destroy the wisdom of the wise, and bring to nothing the understanding of the prudent...For since, in the wisdom of God, the world through wisdom did not know God, it pleased God through the foolishness of the message preached to save those who believe"* (1 Corinthians 1:19, 21).

The Bible speaks of the "noble Bereans" who, after they had heard the preaching, searched the Scriptures daily to see if these things were true. This lady was like a noble Berean, because although she had been a long-time TM meditator, she was willing to peer out from under TM teachings long enough to take a look at the biblical passage I was showing her. Watching her light up with understanding was very gratifying. Maybe the reason so many people try other spiritual paths is because the only Christianity they know does not center in a real relationship with Jesus Christ, but only in a mental concept of Him. A really crafty devil would make full use of his most powerful tool, a dull and lifeless Christianity.

I used to enjoy going to the free suppers dished up at the church a few blocks from my apartment. Most of the people who stood in line for food there were pretty scruffy-looking street people with unkempt, dirty hair. I often brought food to the church for these people so I felt entitled to eat some of it on occasion. It was while waiting in line for food that a street acquaintance of mine was loudly proclaiming through his missing front teeth that there is no hell and no devil (a common belief among New Agers). I simply pointed out to him the verse that says, "..._For this purpose the Son of God was manifested, that He might destroy the works of the devil_" (1 John 3:8). Suddenly he became very quiet. I never had much luck when I tried to convince people using my own logic. It is the powerful anointing of God that does the convincing, when we let the Scriptures do the talking.

TRAFFIC SCHOOL

As you can see, I could hardly keep myself from telling others about Christ. It was the outpouring of God's Spirit that made the difference in my life and enabled me to do this. Acts 2 tells how the disciples of Jesus had to wait for the baptism of the Holy Spirit that would give them spiritual power to become effective witnesses. I don't think I am especially gifted in preaching or witnessing; in fact before I met Christ I used to detest evangelists. God replaced both the spiritual emptiness and the deceptions in my life with revelatory gifting which was more wonderful than anything I experienced when I was in TM. But the Giver of these gifts is the greatest Gift of all! God even used my red-hot zeal for witnessing during my "probation" in traffic school. Here is an excerpt from my diary:

> Went to traffic school yesterday. Nobody is there 'cause they want to be. The teacher is very ingratiating and he knows as well as everybody else that he's just a big babysitter. We see movies of people slamming their cars into brick walls and getting their legs amputated.

Halfway through an especially boring class last night, I looked around and saw a girl next to me reading a book on astrology. People all over the classroom were reading things under the table, whispering, or just enduring the boredom. The Lord kept prompting me to hand a "Jesus Will Be Your Shepherd" tract to the girl next to me. I said, "Here, read this." She did but gave it back to me. I told her, "You can keep it if you want." Instead, she handed it to the next girl who started reading the tract, and guess what? She passed it to the person next to her. And so it went on down the line, and up the next row until it reached a guy near the front who had been asking questions about the effect pot has on your driving. Suddenly, he declared loudly for all to hear, "Get high on the Lord!" Pleased to have gotten peoples' attention, he passed the tract to a guy in the front row who handed it to a truck driver who said, "Get rid of this, why don't ya?" Eventually the tract made its way back to the girl two seats down from me, who stuck it in her book to keep. I couldn't have gotten all that to happen if I'd tried. God gets all the credit. And it goes to show, when you're bored, you'll read anything. Hallelujah!

I didn't want to forget reaching out to my former boyfriend, Rick. So I shared with him how I had found Christ. God's love just overcame me, and if anything happened, it was mostly in the form of tears of love and compassion. I sat for a long time and just wept, and he sat without judging me, knowing I deeply cared for him. He told me that a friend of his who had taken part in the nuclear bomb experiments in the Pacific Ocean had seen a vision of the return of Christ appearing in the fireball in the sky. So, he had some food for thought. Later, I sent him a copy of the *Spiritual Counterfeits Project Journal*, which he said he really liked.

INFANT ZEAL

I was an embarrassment to my family and others during this time in my life. I had lots of zeal, but not much knowledge, wisdom, or *restraint*. In restaurants I would frequently turn around in my chair and start telling the person behind me all about Jesus and ask if they were "saved." A friend of mine named Sylvia and I used to lovingly "stalk" cars in parking lots. I remember poking our heads through one lady's open car window and asking her if she went to church. She replied, "No, but are you all right?" God was very patient with me even if some others were not.

The incredible power and awesome supernatural experiences given to Christian believers must be one of the best-kept secrets because none of us in the New Age movement ever heard of it—we thought we had a corner on spiritual experiences. Well, we had supernatural experiences all right, but usually they were of a different kind of spirit. If you believe the Biblical account could be correct, you will have to consider its claims that there are only two sources of supernatural power—God and Lucifer. The Bible says to "earnestly desire the best gifts...." It was my blessed experience to discover that once I truly gave my heart to the Lord, He was only too happy to give me spiritual gifts as He saw fit.

Soon I was heavily involved in helping many who were caught in the same kind of darkness in which I had previously been entrapped. I would pray for the Lord to send me one person a day and sometimes He sent more than that! I had the "first love" zeal and was very focused on the Lord. I ate an all-raw food diet, which is not bad at all, and I was wearing all white and beads. My attire and eating habits helped my friend Sean and myself to get into a lot of ashrams and meditation centers where we did a little subtle recruiting, and quite a few people were saved. (We also got booted out of a few places.)

In spite of all these incongruities, I did benefit from some of the new ideas Sean brought into my life. A side benefit of knowing Sean was his knowledge of healthy eating. One day he came into the kitchen from his trip to the health food store and plunked down several bags of raw fruits, vegetables, and nuts at the peak of perfection. Then he brought out a bag of fresh wheat grass for juicing. He taught us to eat a totally raw diet, which I did for at least a year. He also instructed us in a lot of other healthy practices. Now I use 60-75% raw food in my diet, as overall it seems to work better. An all-raw diet made me too thin. Thankfully I did not throw out the baby with the bath water (discard all Sean's health practices) when he and I eventually parted ways. As I learned to listen to the Holy Spirit's guidance in all things, including how to stay healthy, I was able to pull myself out of several life-threatening conditions years later and regain my strength.

Even though God used us, I have since repented of my partnering with Sean. The Bible's injunction that two cannot "walk together" unless they are "agreed" proved true in our case. And the mixture Sean still carried of Christianity and Eastern mysticism was something I could not understand. Though I searched in depth, I could not locate any scriptural basis for it.

One of the places where we "recruited" for Jesus was the Living Love Center. If you are really serious about being a witness for the Lord, you sometimes have to have a love of adventure and enjoy challenges. We did not know it when we first got there, but we soon found out that the people were nudists. We were standing in the kitchen, when a couple blithely walked down the stairs, completely naked. We are told to be all things to all men. (No, we did not disrobe.) So we struck up a conversation with the couple. They were so hungry to know God that within a very short time, both of them had received Christ, began attending a church in Berkeley and eventually got married. There are no impossible cases, but you might have to go through some pretty amazing experiences to win them. Be creative. You sometimes have to overlook people's obvious faults for a while in order to see beyond them to their ultimate deliverance.

In one meditation center, I brought along a picture of Jesus I had drawn and asked them if they would like to know Him. Since most of them were familiar with meditation, they did not object when asked to join with Sean and me in calling on the "Name above all names, Jesus." We would sit in a circle and join hands and call out to Jesus together. In one of these encounters, a girl started weeping profusely, whereupon she got up and walked away totally transformed. Often the Lord touched them deeply and delivered them that way. Jesus is very creative in His desire to reach the lost.

"Calling on the name of the Lord" (one of the most frequently mentioned but overlooked phrases in the Bible) brought me to know Him, but it should not be seen as some kind of magic technique for reaching God. The ongoing Christian life involves a deep commitment, and later my prayer time consisted of much more worship and intercession. Still, I often invoke His powerful Name because it quiets me and centers me on Him when other things are trying to steal my attention. For some scriptures that refer to calling on the Name of the Lord, please see the page on the *Name of God* at the end of this book.

After becoming more closely knit with my church, I moved into a small apartment building owned by them. It was located next to the main meeting place on College Avenue just blocks away from the Berkeley campus. Sean was a frequent visitor in those days, attending church with me, trying to live for Christ, but failing to let go of all the intriguing New Age pathways he had traveled. He would take me to various places ostensibly to witness for Christ, but he could never shake their influence on him. Once in a while, Sean would have a breakthrough recommitment to Christ as Savior, complete with tears of repentance. At these times he would say that he felt so much closer to the Lord and to me, even discussing the possibility of our getting married. But then it would all come crashing down as he veered off in another direction, always restless and searching. Furthermore, my heart broke even more every time he turned back.

Sean and I attended a meeting in which Mario Murillo preached about men who falsely build up a woman's expectations, and how this betrayal of trust often leaves scars that last a lifetime. Sean didn't like hearing this truth, so he got up and left before the talk ended, but I knew that the Lord was dealing with him. Maybe part of his temptation was ego because his extraordinary psychic and occult powers won him much adulation and praise from his followers.

While Sean recognized that I had been given a spiritual rebirth through Christ, he still tried to get me to look into other spiritual paths—as if my new life in Christ weren't enough! I gave up trying to figure this out. Perhaps my Christianity seemed too simple to Sean, or maybe it offended him intellectually. You have to be willing just to come to God like a child. It is humbling to be "saved," because you have to admit that you cannot save yourself.

It takes courage to admit one's hopeless condition without Christ and to be willing to trust Him completely.

UNEASY MIXTURES

Most of Sean's ventures outside of the Christian faith involved hybrid Christian-Eastern mystical organizations like Yogananda, Christananda and The Holy Order of Mans. Sean chose to ignore the many Biblical incongruities in the teachings of these groups. The Christananda Center was very beautiful. Their simple meditation-prayer chamber was long and empty except for some green plants and an intense yellow rug. I discovered that their leader had been touched by Jesus, so I shared with some of the people who ran their bookstore how the very accessible presence of Jesus can move one to tears of joy. They expressed a longing to experience His presence, so I encouraged them to read the Bible and to hunger and seek after the Lord.

Many of these Christian offshoots were rather subtle and deceiving. Their leaders would mention Jesus Christ to lend credibility, only to depart in some disastrous way from what Jesus actually taught. When I confronted the leader and founder of Christananda how Christianity and yoga don't mix, I was told to lay aside my "fears" and to be more "open-minded" and tolerant of the attempts of others to reach God. While I am not opposed to sincere spiritual seeking, I do feel that many people have distorted the simple Gospel. Jesus taught very clearly against changing and mixing the Gospel with other traditions to make it more "palatable."

11

Boot Camp

WISDOM, TIMING, AND COMPASSION

*D*uring those early days the Lord allowed my experiences with Sean at the ashrams and meditation centers to strengthen my understanding of the difference between the Christian faith and the claims of other spiritual groups. It was quite a boot camp! These fledgling forays into uncharted waters might have derailed my new understanding, but I was able to recognize God's sovereignty and unquenchable purpose through it all. One day Sean went to Los Angeles to visit the ashram of the little boy guru from India, Maharaji, who had a huge following and performed many signs and miracles. He claimed to be "higher than God." I was incredulous that Sean could not see through this absurd lie. Concerned, I drove all the way down to L.A. in one day to see if I could "rescue" him from this deception.

I spent the night on the floor in my sleeping bag. The room was jam-packed with hundreds of Maharaji followers, all high from days of chanting and meditating. I felt like a friendly counter-spy. During the night, a stealthy spirit came up to me and whispered in my ear, "My name is very pure." I immediately recognized that it was a lying spirit and rebuked it in Jesus' name, and it left.

As a new Christian, I felt secure in the covering of prayer. Also, I could sense the power and protection of the blood of Christ, which He promises to those who place their trust in Him. Those who follow human gurus cannot know God's protection in the same way as those who are "bought" by the precious blood of Christ. That is our uniqueness and sets us apart from other paths. We must realize that not all spirits are interested in the welfare of humans. We also must know that our own strength is no match for them. There is only One who is greater in power than any of the false and deceiving spirits in the heavens, and that is Christ who defeated all principalities and powers by the Cross. As this was my understanding at the time I visited the ashrams, I went with complete confidence. However, it is always wise to discern the Lord's leading before undertaking such things and to go with a friend for extra prayer covering. This is a good approach to follow at all times in spiritual matters.

Before leaving for home the next day, I spent some time sitting with a small cell group of Maharaji devotees on the lawn and sharing my knowledge of Jesus with them. I confronted a man about the many lies and falsehoods I felt had trapped him. He called my vehemence and passionate zeal for the truth "hate" and said that if Christ were the only way, he would see more love in me. Even though he misunderstood my deep concern for him, it nevertheless caused me to reexamine the manner in which I was presenting Jesus to people oriented toward the New Spirituality. If I had been in his shoes, as indeed I had in times past, listening to someone with an approach like mine probably would have evoked the same reaction.

We must understand that people in other spiritual paths, especially those who are involved in psychic practices, have not yet comprehended the infinite, glorious, and unique dimension of Jesus. They think all spiritual power—both good and evil—stems from the same source. This is a common fallacy. Furthermore, much of their lives are cloaked in the subtleties and disciplines of long hours of solitary meditation. Truly, even though they may be unaware that the Scriptures are absolutely accurate, they are very disciplined in bringing their entire lifestyle into a devotional pattern of living. In fact, it was the beautiful appearance of a devotional lifestyle that had attracted me to these groups in the first place.

Bringing our truth to bear too forcibly and suddenly without considering mental and emotional readiness is like suddenly shining a 10,000 watt spotlight; it is blinding and often misinterpreted. Sometimes even a tiny bit of revelatory knowledge can be like a lightning bolt, so we must go easy and pray for gently applied wisdom, timing, and compassion. Many New Age people are open and interested in what we have to share. Some of my Christian readers may not agree with me, but I feel that at times God speaks to unsaved people—if in no other way, through the vehicle of conscience. Some who are not yet born again may hear from God regularly and love Him passionately, but may not have encountered Him personally! Christians are not the only ones to hear from God. Even in my most lost years, God was speaking to me. Many times I "heard His voice" deep within my being and at times changed my agenda because of these softly, inwardly-spoken, directional cues—lovingly given to me by my Creator. It's just that I did not know Jesus in a very personal way and was still bound in my old nature. I did not have a reborn spirit. However, some in the New Age movement have a profound capacity for spiritual things. If they met the Lord, they probably could go even deeper in their relationship with Him than some lukewarm professing Christians. Often, they show more of a Christlike character than many Christians. Sad but true.

BRIDGE BUILDERS

God has placed in every culture and religion a recognizable bridge by which people can relate to Biblical truth. We bridge gaps every day in order to communicate better with people we'd like to know. It is just common courtesy (love and respect) to do no less for those of other cultures and religious persuasions. Otherwise, the passion that Christians feel for their Savior can be misconstrued and unwittingly cause offense, thus doing more harm than good to the cause of Christ. Many accuse Christians of being uneducated, insensitive, heavy-handed, and politically incorrect. Of course, God can use even bumbling efforts, but we should always move in sensitivity and with real love and concern for the other person. If we are using wisdom we will be able to say with the apostle Paul, *"...I have become all things to all men, that I might by all means save some"* (1 Corinthians 9:22). Wisdom should be our hallmark, because it is our birthright and inheritance.

Many spiritual seekers I have known are caught in a kind of spiritual bankruptcy, but are only dimly aware of it. Some of them are hurting deeply. They try to drown the suspicion of their emptiness with their feelings of meditation-induced bliss, much like an alcoholic's drink. If Christians are genuinely concerned for them, they will see God's love in us. We do not always have to immediately broadcast the source of that love to them. I have found that a fulfilled life, radiating the peace of God, is a Christian's most effective "argument." I've been amazed at the number of people who once sought spiritual life through Eastern meditations coming to Christ because what the Lord Jesus Christ has to offer is unmatchable.

COUNTENANCE OF LOVE

It was the beautiful, serene, authentic countenance of a Christian woman I met at a party that drew my attention to Christ. She was the sister-in-law of one of my TM teacher friends. When I asked her if she was a transcendental meditator, she said "No," but then she told me of her encounter with Jesus and how He had transformed her life. I believed her. The influence of an outward demeanor reflecting the inward grace of Christ is a powerful witness. The effect of this witness depends on the spiritual condition of the observer. There was a time when just seeing a Christian acquaintance downtown would have sent me to the other side of the street to avoid the possibility of having to talk with them. An interesting Bible scripture puts it aptly: _"For we are to God the aroma of Christ among those who are being saved and those who are perishing. To the one we are the smell of death; to the other, the fragrance of life"_ (2 Corinthians 2:15, NIV).

Many Christians are afraid to speak about their faith because they suppose that they will be rejected. But if they really trust God and leave the results up to Him, why should it matter? I was my most rejecting, persecuting self toward Christians just a few days before I encountered Him. Sometimes, immediately before someone finds Christ, their old human nature will stage one final, desperate refusal to relinquish its hold on them. Their ensuing tantrum can get quite extreme, like death throes. But God's power can act as a shield to fully protect a believer if they should run up against these reactions in others.

The light of truth has a powerful way of exposing our deeply held prejudices. There was a group of Christians that met on the campus regularly, and though I criticized them to Sean, he made no comments. A few days later, I saw them standing together near the Student Union singing praises to God. What spoke louder than words, was their powerful unity that went beyond the merely obvious. Each individual seemed filled with the same, unseen living Presence. They were like those described in Isaiah 7:2, *"So his heart and the heart of his people were moved as the trees of the woods are moved with the wind."* This beautiful manifestation of joy and unity was what eventually disarmed my animosity and left me open to Christ.

The Lord was very patient with me in my new spiritual infancy as I began to be introduced to a life of true discipleship. Sean, rootless soul that he was, took up residence on the back porch of my apartment in the former "Resurrection City" church building where I was living with two other women. With his winsome personality, he often tried to distract me at church meetings by whispering in my ear and making jokes. Finally, a fellow staff member who lived on the second floor of our apartment building told me that she felt Sean should move out of the back porch room to *"abstain from all appearance of evil"* (1 Thessalonians 5:22 KJV). So I asked him to leave and explained why. It wasn't long before he began to have a few affairs with women, even though he continued to see me. This confused and upset me a lot, but I still clung to the hope that he would soon change and see the light.

LEI LADY LEI

Sean continued to refuse to acknowledge Jesus as Master of his life. I agonized in bewilderment at how he could lead me to God and still not know God! The Bible warns about double-minded people who serve the Lord AND at the same time follow after their idols. Basically, Sean refused to trust *Christ alone.* But Jesus is like a jealous lover. He loves us too much to be willing to share His glory with another. If you think about it, do we need to look further once we have found the Source of absolute beauty and perfection?

One day when at Sean's apartment, I saw a book on Tantric (sexual) yoga. Yoga technically means "union with God." However, it is not the spiritual union a believer grows into with Christ, but it is about psychic energies and forces and spiritual seduction. Often books like these will attempt to "substantiate" their error with verses from the Bible taken out of context. Earlier on I would have thought all spiritual paths were legitimate. But I discovered that Jesus has nothing whatsoever to do with Tantric yoga. I was greatly upset with Sean and demanded honesty. When I opened the refrigerator door a Hare Krishna lei fell out.

Sean said, "Put it on; it will deliver you from 1,000 years of bad karma." I responded to him honestly, "No thanks, Christ has already delivered me by dying on a cross for me. What can compare with the costly blood of our Creator? Can a perishable lei give eternal life? If this were so, Jesus would not have had to suffer agony and death on the cross for me."

GENTLY FLOWING OR RAGING?

Sean wasn't a famous yogi like Maharaji or Maharishi, but I knew that he had powerful psychic abilities. Once during a discussion about the strong and unusual manifestations of Guru Maharaji, Sean said that some of the experiences were "passed on." He then asked me to go into the next room and count to three. I did so, and at the count of three, an enormous, brilliant flash of light hit me squarely between the eyes and almost knocked me to the floor. From the living room I could hear him wildly laughing and saying, "Did you see it?"

Sean believed that he could raise my level of consciousness by applying psychic energy to the top of my head through the pressure of his hand. This manipulation was an attempt to draw up the *kundalini*, or "serpent force." Making the kundalini rise up within their followers is one of the favorite pastimes of the gurus. When this power is "awakened," it supposedly rises up the spine all the way to the top of the cranium, causing a heightened state of consciousness. After I was filled with God's Holy Spirit, I often experienced jerking motions, as this lawless "serpent power" came in conflict with the power within me and would begin to descend back down the spine. Sean knew what was happening, and at one point he said he would make it go down once and for all. After a moment of intense concentration, Sean said that it was "down" for good. I did feel this force abate and never experienced it again. At the same time, Sean said that he was permanently cutting off all spiritual ties between the Maharishi and me. I now believe that all credit goes to God for this separation from the previous occult activity in my life.

Once when I was in the bathroom fixing my hair, I made a certain face in the mirror, checked myself out thoroughly as women do, and then went outside to join Sean and some other friends. Sean said, "How did you look in the mirror?" He gave a big laugh and then proceeded to make the same kind of funny face at me that

I had just made in the mirror. I was not only embarrassed, but annoyed by such an invasion of my privacy.

Psychic experience is totally different from the kind of manifestation the Holy Spirit imparts. According to Scripture, the Spirit of the Lord is gentle, peaceable, easy to be entreated, and full of good fruits (James 3:17). The Bible describes the difference between the "gently flowing waters of Shiloh" and the "raging waters of the Euphrates" (Isaiah 8). Although this passage refers to the Assyrian army, it makes me think of the difference between the Holy Spirit and psychic power. The Lord is strong and mighty, but He doesn't need to force anyone to receive from Him. However, I can attest that once you have tasted of His love, you will never be the same. No other guru, technique, or religion will ever satisfy you once Jesus has touched your life. The Bible even calls following any other way a form of spiritual "adultery."

DEVOURING WOLF

I did not always believe in hell. There are many reasons why I do believe in it now. I hope that after reading this book, both heaven and hell will seem more real to you. A little glimpse of hell never hurt anybody—it can go a long way in keeping one on the straight and narrow! Although being warned about hell never made heaven seem more inviting to me, hearing about the joys and gifts of the Holy Spirit whetted my appetite. Indeed, after having tasted the gifts, I never wanted to risk losing them.

During my pre-Christian days my friends and I found a Christian poster on campus warning people about the reality of hell. I admit it was kind of a ridiculous poster. We put it up on the wall of my apartment and loved to laugh at it. Since then my outlook has done a complete turnabout. Even though the artwork on this poster was a bit hokey, the message was still valid: heaven and hell are real. Unfortunately, this concept generally has not been accepted in modern culture, but this seems to be changing. To draw on Pascal's famous wager, it won't hurt you to believe what the Bible says about hell. What about the reverse? Many are beginning to count the cost of their unbelief.

Sean was one who did not think that anyone would ever wind up in hell. One day while I was visiting him, the Lord gave me a vision. In this vision, he looked like a vicious, devouring wolf. At that time, I was unfamiliar with the Biblical teaching about false prophets who attempt to deceive the flock by wearing sheep's clothes, but are inwardly "ravenous wolves." When I shared what I had seen with Sean, it made him extremely nervous. However, he was unwilling to change.

The Scriptures are full of warnings about deceivers and liars. Consider these verses from the Bible:

You will know them by their fruits.

(Matthew 7:16)

The thief does not come except to steal, and to kill, and to destroy.

(John 10:10)

He [Satan] *is a liar and the father of it.*

(John 8:44)

For this purpose the Son of God was manifested, that He might destroy the works of the devil.

(I John 3:8)

Sean had already ripped me off financially by getting me to sell off all of my household effects at an apartment garage sale. He said it was an opportunity to give up my material possessions "for the Lord," just as they did in the early Church. Under the pretext of using the money for "ministry work," he then bought himself three sets of clothes and a lot of other things. Months later, when we were in the bank he flipped me a few bills, but it hardly covered the amount I had given him. However, I was able to find the grace not to hold a grudge.

Sean seemed very paranoid at times, slept with a rifle in his bed every night, and would hint that there were some people who were "after" him for money that he owed them. Once we went to look at some land with the intention of possibly buying some acreage for a "Christian retreat." While we were sitting on top of one of the mountains, Sean told me to be very quiet and to listen to the "sound of the universe." Immediately, I began to hear a distinct humming noise, which grew steadily louder and went on for quite a long time. It sounded like the vibration of a gigantic, primordial motor permeating everything from the lower depths of the earth to the enormous expanse of the sky. However, for some reason, it also sounded and felt very evil. Sean told me that it was the universal "aum" sound upon which people chant and meditate. Although the "aum" mantra is commonly chanted, I now realize that this sound came from the demonic realm to deceive me. When we started down the mountainside, I kept seeing branches of trees on the ground that resembled horns. At first I couldn't believe my eyes, but the more I looked, the more "horns" I saw scattered everywhere. It gave me a sinister, creepy feeling and made me want to get out of there fast. I mentioned it to Sean, but he didn't say anything. I knew I was being warned not to return to that land and certainly not to buy it.

Much later, in a rare moment of honesty, he confessed that he had intended to purchase the land (with my money) and then to sell the property for his own gain. With all these incidents, one would think I finally would have gotten the picture. But I just couldn't reconcile his intentionally deceiving me, because after all, hadn't he led me to God? It took a lot to get me to realize that spiritual experiences are not a litmus test of good character. I knew that Jesus was trustworthy, but I began to have serious doubts about Sean.

One of the times I came the closest to becoming spiritually derailed was the time that Sean took me to the San Francisco's "Holy Order of Mans." This group believed in meditation, long hours of charity work, and a disciplined lifestyle to get to "enlightenment." Sean introduced me to one of their leaders so that I could describe my salvation experience to him and why I thought that Jesus was the only way to heaven. The leader tried to explain to me that Easterners are spiritually "wired" differently from Westerners. He asserted that they need to go through their own gurus and masters. His one concession to Christianity was that eventually everybody would have to enter heaven through Jesus Christ—the narrow gate—even though many different spiritual paths lead to that gate. I found this partial truth very confusing.

SPIRITUAL RESIDUE

The Lord showed great forbearance with me during my much-too-long association with Sean. If I had known what I know today, I would have paid heed to the scripture,

Therefore come out from among them and be separate, says the Lord. Do not touch what is unclean, and I will receive you. I will be a Father to you. And you shall be My sons and daughters, says the Lord Almighty.
(2 Corinthians 6:17-18)

In spite of my stubbornness, God did bring a good measure of deliverance to me during my time with Sean.

As long as our hearts desire to follow God completely, He will always, sooner or later, sift out from our lives those things that hinder our progress. I discovered years later that teaming up with Sean had left an unseen spiritual residue. If you walk through a bramble patch, you shouldn't be surprised that you pick up a few stickers. If you sit in a room full of cigarette smoke, you shouldn't wonder why your hair smells like smoke. I had picked up a spiritual residue that would not just "go away" without deeper repentance, cleansing, and deliverance counseling. Notice that although Jesus reached out with compassion to the multitudes, He did not form close, intimate associations with those who practice deceit. This is because He is holy. The wrong kind of close soul ties can cause a crossover into our lives of things we would not welcome.

CREATIVE WORSHIP

My experience with Sean taught me to be careful of counterfeit manifestations, not only in other religions, but in the church as well. We must pray for discernment. I have noticed an unfortunate trend among some respected Christian leaders to debunk supernatural manifestations just because they seem "New Agey." Jan Kuby, one of my former roommates and a former follower of Sean's, noticed some people worshipping their guru while doing hand dances in the air. After Jan became born-again and was attending an inspired and anointed Christian gathering, she saw what appeared to be similar hand motions, only they were worshipping Christ. She aptly concurred that the form was similar, but it was not the same nor was it similarly inspired.

We should stop criticizing the way others worship, and focus on Jesus Himself. I think that Jesus really delights in the hand dancing done for Him. The reason Christians tend to have much greater joy is that they have been adopted as sons and daughters of the Creator. They talk with Him and hear from Him in a divine and joyful two-way exchange. Look how Jesus expresses His diverse creativity through all the forms of color and beauty in nature—e.g., flowers, birds, mountains, lakes—placed on this earth for our enjoyment. It's not surprising that He would welcome many forms of worship as well. A dry and expressionless Christianity would not reflect the pure joy and love of Christ, nor would it convince the skeptic.

GOD HAS SOME STRANGE KIDS

What happens when your church is invaded by a troop of God-hungry yogis dressed in white sheets? How would you react to some street kids wearing blue mohawk hairstyles and sporting pierced body parts? Some of you might say, "Cool." When my friend Jan Kuby came to Christ, she was a member of a commune of spiritual seekers who lived up on a mountain and wore nothing but white sheets. When they and their leader found Christ through a miraculous series of circumstances, they wound up at a church that did not accept the way they dressed. Eventually, another church received them fully with the love of Jesus. If anybody was troubled by the way they dressed, they prayed about it privately. Let's face it, some of God's kids seem weird. Some of you reading this book look really strange, and you like it that way. That's okay. If God wants you to look different, He will let you know.

When the Lord began to speak to those in Jan's group that He wanted them to change their style of dress, one by one they began to graduate from the white bed sheets to "normal" clothes. He tailors His instructions uniquely for each person. He doesn't want us all looking like Barbie and Ken dolls. I recall how Jesus took delight in showing me how He wanted me to dress. I really loved that. He would pick out which clothes in my closet He preferred me to wear. He also showed me where to find really nice clothes at special bargains. It's similar to a husband telling his wife how he really likes to see her dressed. Jesus is our heavenly Bridegroom, and He wants us to look nice.

What is normal appearance to one person may be strange to another. We need to accept people with the unconditional love of Jesus Christ and not judge them by their looks or their dress. Otherwise, we will lose some of God's precious individuals. The church that judged Jan and her friends lost their fellowship.

What if God allows some of his children to wear a Mohawk or a nose ring? He could be testing our attitude, you know. Perhaps He intends to later send that one into a pack of street people to witness to them about the plan of salvation. God is God. We must be open to what He is doing these days.

THE GRAND LIE

Christians (even really intelligent ones) can be deceived if they are not really familiar with the Bible "road map." Jan was a good example of this. Even though later she completed her Ph.D. in biochemistry and obtained a tenured professorship at the University of San Francisco, she was not immune from Sean's spiritual deception. The wilderness testing experiences following my conversion would have been enough to get most people thoroughly confused or lost, if it had not been for my daily familiarity with the teachings of the Bible. These scriptures attuned me to hear the voice of the Holy Spirit, our great Friend and Guide. That guidance proved itself to be a real anchor to me again and again and a *"light unto my path"* (Psalm 119:105). The Lord was a faithful and true Shepherd to me during this time and has proven Himself to me over and over again without exception.

GREENER PASTURES

As the light of the glorious Gospel of Christ grew steadily brighter in my life, Sean's influence grew dimmer as he began to fade from the scene. He got tired of being discovered and harangued and finally left for greener pastures. I had not yet learned the art of truly resting in Christ and casting all my care upon Him. Although we can influence others, only God can produce the needed changes. Also, I should have ended the relationship much sooner. Later, I had a strange dream in which I saw Sean setting himself up on a kind of throne in a large auditorium, where a dozen or more people were bowing down to him and paying homage. He shared his throne with a special guest of honor, a street celebrity and acquaintance of mine who only wore white and claimed that he lived exclusively on raw wheat grass and wheat berries. (Actually, I never did see him eat anything but grass. He would chew it and then spit out the pulp.)

This dream seemed to come true as I met up with some of Sean's followers by chance. They were preparing to have a meeting honoring him as their psychic guru. In the ladies' restroom, one of the young women was talking about Sean, her new boyfriend and guru. They were in a hurry to leave, so I did not have an opportunity to warn them. That was also the last time that I ever saw Sean, but I prayed that some day he would be able to trust Christ fully and find total freedom and integrity.

SECRET KNOWLEDGE AND THE END TIMES

When Jesus walked on this earth, He warned about the deception of the end times that would occur through the signs and wonders performed by those claiming to be Christ. The New Spirituality will appear beautiful and full of wisdom, but lead many astray. If you have a problem with believing the Bible as I once did, you might be opening yourself to the deception of which Jesus spoke. We see an example of deception in Genesis 3:5-6 when the serpent, Satan, came to Eve in the Garden of Eden and promised, _"...your eyes will be opened, and you will be like God, knowing **good** and evil"_ (emphasis on _'good'_). How many times have we missed it because we were blinded by our own opinions or someone else's _good_ intentions? The good sometimes can be the enemy of the best. God was offering an exclusive wisdom from the superior realm of His infinite storehouse of knowledge. But when Eve saw that the tree was _"**good** for food, and that it was pleasant to the eyes and a tree to be desired to make one wise,"_ she disobeyed God and ate the fruit, and Adam also ate it. They settled for what was immediate, easy and natural and lost what was immortal and _supernatural_. In 1 John 2:16-17 we read: _"For all that is in the world—the lust of the flesh_ ('good for food'), _the lust of the eyes_ ('pleasant to the eyes'), _and the pride of life_ ('to make one wise')—_is not of the Father, but is of the world. And the world is passing away, and the lust of it; but he who does the will of God abides forever."_

It is important to realize that, from the beginning, there was an extremely powerful spirit called "Lucifer" who rebelled and determined to counterfeit the plan of God. The "grand lie" can be seen from Genesis through early Babylonian times to its final showdown in "Mystery Babylon" spoken of in the book of Revelation. The heart of this lie is spiritual seduction to worship the autonomous self. Its powers are disguised as "secret knowledge" presented as "God-realization." Satan can duplicate some of the spiritual gifts, but not divine love.

Even when I was involved with TM, I had misgivings about the concept of *karma;* it seemed extremely self-centered. In India today few will reach out to the very poor and wretched ones who lie in the streets hungry and neglected. They believe that the poor were born into that life because of sins in their past lives. Therefore, little or nothing is done to alleviate their suffering. This view of life is devoid of the mercy, compassion, and forgiveness that Jesus taught His disciples. When Maharishi was asked by a cynical member in his audience how TM would help the poor in India, Maharishi gave this astounding reply: *"They will be hungry, but they will be happy."*[10] This may break the record as one of the most underwhelming statements of all time by an alleged enlightened master.

Understanding the Bible provides a reliable standard as to the truthfulness of any philosophy. To be specific, if one desires to live by a philosophy or a belief system, one should know where it stands with regard to God, man, and sin. Many signs and wonders can be deceptive in their ability to mimic some of the supernatural miracles of God. A Biblical account of this is in Exodus when Pharoah's magicians were able to duplicate many of the feats of Moses, but they did not have the covering of the blood of the Lamb over their doorposts as did the Israelites. As the destroying angel passed over their homes, only those under the blood covering were spared. This blood foreshadowed the covenant blood of Christ (the Lamb of God) and was the only provision given for their deliverance from harm.

To summarize, we should ask ourselves, "How would the story of this account apply to us today?" In the *"strong delusion"* spoken of in 2 Thessalonians 2:11, it would seem that only those who are covered by this blood will have the spiritual discernment needed to distinguish the true from the false in these awesome and challenging last days. And if we think that we are capable of this discernment through our own innate understanding, we may need to guard ourselves from the error of pride.

12

Desire of the Ancients

COMMON GROUND

*S*piritual experiences alone without a firm knowledge of the Bible and a close, intimate relationship with God are insufficient barometers of spiritual attainment. If this book enables you to see this, you'll know a lot more than all the gurus, "enlightened" masters, and even quite a few Christians. If we have been given gifts of the Spirit, it is all the more important that we walk humbly. Otherwise we may fall into the same trap of pride that deceived Lucifer before the creation of this world. We must continually examine ourselves in the light of the Scriptures and allow ourselves to be led daily by the Holy Spirit. At the very least, we must avoid being lulled into a complacency that would rob us of our full inheritance.

If God gives you dreams and visions, it does not make you more "spiritual" than others. Although it is a bit unusual, it is just another gift, like teaching or healings. I feel sure that the Lord promised me I would one day move in the gift of miracles. But at first I needed deliverance from my past, cleaning out the old in order to bring in the new. The Lord prepared me for this by giving me an insatiable hunger to know more about God and to know Him personally. I spent many hours studying the Bible, bathing in its glorious truths, and letting Him work a mighty reshaping and renewing of my mind. Each revelation was like another piece fitting into a gigantic puzzle. Everything became more clear. I also began spending much time in prayer and Christian meditation, as well as occasionally fasting—another great spiritual tool. I have to say that even now my hunger for God and His revealed Word just keeps getting richer and deeper.

Soon I discovered that Christians of all ages, educational levels, and social backgrounds were experiencing this overflowing life. Some were experiencing the miraculous. Others seemed happy without these supernatural experiences. It astounds me that I had not known about this path sooner. Today the Lord is weaving many different kinds of Christians into His tapestry. Indeed, down throughout the centuries the Church has played an important part in forming our rich and diverse cultural heritage. When I look within the historic Church and see that there have been many creative Christians, even geniuses, such as Bach, Pascal, Rembrandt, Dickens, T. S. Eliot, and Tolstoy, I've had to repent of ever thinking that church people are not very creative or smart. Christianity is truly a cross-section of humanity.

The amazing thing is that such a diverse crowd has managed to attain a certain degree of cohesiveness. The reason for this is a matter of changed focus—looking beyond themselves to the superior excellence and power of Christ. *This is the true ego loss that people on Eastern paths can only dream about.* Thus, rather than obliterating the ego to escape its demands (as Eastern paths frequently advocate), Christianity "saves" the ego (and fulfills it) by bringing it into proper submission to its Creator.

Another TM initiator came to Christ around the time that I did. This educated man said that he had reached the state of "cosmic-consciousness" and had begun to experience "God-consciousness." When some Christians pointed out to him the plan of salvation, he asked God for a sign. He asked that if Jesus were really the only way to God, he would be stricken with an incurable disease. (Those in TM believe that once you reach these states of consciousness, you are perfect and cannot get sick.) He immediately came down with cancer. Although everyone in our church prayed for his healing, he never recovered health in this life. Since I had believed so earnestly for God to heal him, my faith was shaken for a while, but the fact that he faced death as a very completed and utterly peaceful man spoke volumes to me. _"Precious in the eyes of the Lord is the death of his saints"_ (Psalm 116:15).

PSYCHIC AND SPIRITUAL
Knowing the Difference

Great confusion abounds concerning psychic phenomena versus true spiritual experiences. They are commonly thought to be the same. When I was involved in Eastern paths I used to view spiritual power as a kind of neutral force to be used and controlled like tapping into electricity. This ocean of power is often referred to as the "collective unconscious." Many think that all religions tap into this same pool of energy. Adherents usually do not believe, even when warned, that what they are contacting is not some vast, neutral, spiritual force-field, but the realm of fallen spirits or demons.

One only needs to observe two year old children to recognize that human beings are rebellious by nature. We do not like to acknowledge that there is a personal God greater than ourselves because it implies our need to worship and serve Him. But as Bob Dylan's song goes, "You've got to serve somebody." The greatest error, the one that caused Lucifer to fall in the beginning, was the sin of pride or self-exaltation. Those who have allowed something other than God to fill the position reserved only for Him have become linked with Satan instead of God. This shocking state of affairs is no less true just because someone is ignorant of it. Leviticus 5:17 says, *"If a person sins, and commits any of these things which are forbidden to be done by the commandments of the Lord, though he does not know it, yet he is guilty and shall bear his iniquity."* The sinner had to bring a trespass offering to the priest for an atonement even though the sin was committed in ignorance. Today, this atonement is available through the blood of Jesus Christ. When we come to Him, our slate is wiped clean and we can have a brand new start. This is why it is called "The Good News!"

There are many different ways a person can be lured into a spiritually independent mindset. Once this foothold is accomplished, dark spiritual influences can then exert more and more control over their thoughts and life, even giving them considerable psychic powers. This is how the gurus and the psychics obtain their power. This is probably why some of those practicing Transcendental Meditation and yoga experience drastic personality changes. We must be aware that there are only *two* sources of spiritual power—God and Lucifer.

The world is beginning to want to know more about the devil and the deceptive role he is playing in these last days. However, this subject makes some people uncomfortable because they think we shouldn't be focusing on evil spirits. I would have to agree with you! While we need to focus primarily on God, there still remains a great need to identify the problem and power of demonic strongholds. We also need to understand the conflict in order to successfully deal with it. Going into a state of denial is not the answer.

The Bible indicates that there are three differing levels of heaven. The first heaven is the natural, visible sky that surrounds our world. The second heaven, I believe, is the psychic or soulish realm inhabited by fallen spirits. The third heaven is the spirit realm of God and the holy angels. Please accept my definition for purposes of this discussion. I believe there is scriptural justification for it. The Bible says that God by His Word has created a great divide between soul and spirit. *"For the word of God is living and powerful, and sharper than any two-edged sword, piercing even to the division of soul and spirit, and of joints and marrow, and is a discerner of the thoughts and intents of the heart"* (Hebrews 4:12).

Man is a tripartite being—spirit, soul, and body. Notice how this reflects the tripartite nature of God himself as Father, Son, and Holy Spirit. The soul of man refers to the mind, will, and emotions. If the soul of man is not wholly given to God, it can become a "playing field" for fallen spirits.

How did fallen spirits come into our world in the first place? In the beginning, Satan was expelled from the realm of God because he rebelled against God's rule and authority, wanting "to be God." He was given the possibility of influencing the will of the first humans by offering the bait of deceptive values and false happiness. His plan worked! The fallen angels were assigned to the second heaven, or psychic realm. Since they could not "be God," they devised a plan to influence and penetrate the natural (or soul) realm with the ultimate intention of possessing those made in God's image. Through progressive deceptions and temptations, their plan was gradually to gain more and more power over their victims until they became their slaves.

Prior to the fall of man, Adam and Eve were able to see the Spirit realm to enjoy God and fellowship with Him. But when they disobeyed God and ate fruit from the forbidden tree of knowledge, their relationship of trust with God was broken and their spirit ceased to be immortal. Death entered the picture. No longer was true happiness and a blissful life in eternity automatically theirs. Because the Original Sin was passed down through the generations, spiritual perception became greatly limited. In man's unregenerate state, he no longer could be trusted with spiritual power.

But what attraction was so irresistible that they succumbed to its influence? They had everything they could ever desire in the paradise of God. They excelled in all kinds of spiritual abilities and enjoyed fellowship with God and each other. In fact, they had everything they needed as long as they chose the wisdom and counsel of God above their own selfish desires and the influence of their adversary. Misplaced love caused the tragic fall. Thankfully, God provided a way of restoration. Without spiritual illumination, I would not have believed this if you had told me. We can't fully grasp this truth without "born-again" eyes.

Reconciliation first came through the sacrifices and offerings of the Old Testament and then later, through the one-time, sinless offering of Jesus Christ, the Lamb of God. The blood of sheep and goats was merely a picture or type of the blood of Christ, which alone has the power to cleanse us from all sin. Only through spiritual surrender of faith and obedience to the will of God can men and women now be given true spiritual abilities. Spiritual power used for one's own purposes will wind up using us!

There is a secret to achieving the kind of surrender necessary to fulfill God's will in our lives. Sacrificial internal submission is the highest form of obedience and much more costly than any other kind of sacrifice. As John Paul Jackson of Streams Ministries states, *"To submit, we not only have to lay down our own agenda, but our emotional resistance toward doing another's agenda."[11]* How do we overcome this emotional resistance? It is by loving our Creator. 1 John 4:19 says, *"We love Him, because He first loved us."* But you can't return a divine love you have not yet received. We learn from the Scriptures, *"Ask, and you will receive, that your joy may be full"* (John 16:24).

Many Christians dismiss psychics as having a "false gift." I would like to challenge you to look a little deeper. It should be noted that many of them have an above average inward sensitivity and capacity for prophetic gifts and other spiritual abilities. While they do not yet know the ultimate Source and Giver of life and revelation, they may exhibit a genuine appreciation for and interest in the prophetic. I believe that people generally are drawn toward the things they enjoy. But prophetic ability is like having a satellite "receiver"; apart from God's revelation of truth, inevitably it winds up being switched to another "channel." The equipment that was designed to receive from the Holy Spirit will begin to receive counterfeit information from another spirit, sometimes even *"another Jesus"* (2 Corinthians 11:4). Therefore, those who desire to move in prophetic gifting must be intimately connected with the true Source of spiritual power, or they will operate in what is referred to as a "false gift."

Discerning the difference between natural prophetic capacity and the prophetic gift of the Holy Spirit is similar to understanding "true north" vs. "magnetic north." Given the opportunity, a magnet will align itself with the earth's natural magnetic field, which can vary depending on where you are located. The magnetic pole wanders somewhat over many years. True North on the other hand is stable and very accurate and does not wander around like the earth's magnetic north. It is reliable and trustworthy, and so is God!

Finding True North requires greater effort than locating magnetic north, precisely because its position is not relative, but infinitely precise. Mere human potential cannot encompass the incorruptible, eternal dimension and precision of God. That is why most people settle for what is personally accessible for them, though ultimately flawed, rather than admit their need for God's help (which entails grace and forgiveness). However, if they settle for less, they will never know Jesus, "Light of the World," and will be eternally separated from their divine destiny and ultimate perfection. There must be a deliberate surrender of the will to His sovereignty and an acknowledgment of the absolute need for Him. God will then respond, touch their lives, and bring the great Paradigm Shift or transformation—a reborn, pure, and yielded heart.

Mere verbal assent to the will of God cannot bring new life. It's not as easy as tapping a kaleidoscope for another configuration. Eternal transformation sometimes comes only after an intense and prolonged search for ultimate answers. Once the "critical mass" of spiritual hunger is reached, breakthrough can be rapid. But death to self (relinquishing control to God) usually begins slowly from within the silent sanctuary of the human heart. Final surrender to the Lordship of Christ then becomes the pivotal spiritual event of a person's lifetime. The gift of our trust in God's superior wisdom is what touches His face and moves His heart toward us. Knowing God, experiencing His cleansing, and walking in revelatory power is worth any cost. It is the pearl of great price.

WAR IN THE HEAVENS

One of the rudest shocks to hit me after I was born-again was the realization that I had been thrust right into the middle of a spiritual war. Although Jesus won this war for us when He suffered on the cross, we still have to walk out our own salvation with great respect and awe (Philippians 2:12). There are many casualties in this war. If you don't know that you are involved in a war, it's not likely that you will win. And how can you win if you can't perceive your heavenly Commander? We must come to a place in our spiritual lives where our communication with God goes both ways, or we will lack the power to fight effectively. This is very crucial, and for some reason many people do not see its absolute importance.

The Bible says that Satan comes to kill, steal, or destroy our rightful inheritance. He is the quintessential rip-off artist. If he cannot win your soul, the next best thing he'd like to do is to dismantle your life, your marriage, your children, your finances and your destiny. He does this by finding some moral weakness or stronghold in your life with which to harass you. If you stop short of becoming filled with the Spirit or if you are ignorant of what the Word of God says is rightfully yours, how will you be able to use your spiritual weapons or recognize the enemy when he comes in all his many subtle forms?

One big mistake people make is to think that one can enter into this war without developing a much deeper one-on-one relationship with the Lord. If as a result of our worship and adoration times we are experiencing the intimate love of the Father, we will automatically have the kind of protection and power necessary to step into the Isaiah 61 anointing that will release the captives and set them free. We "fight" this war not through violence or hate (fleshly human devices), but by yielding everything to God in prayer. Submission to God is not always an easy thing. Human beings tend to enjoy taking matters into their own hands. We love to rule just like He does because we are made in His image. But if we do not yield to His will, our hearts will be divided. For those who surrender unconditionally, great victories can be won. Many New Agers have seen a superior love and greater power in Christianity than in their own movement, and God has made them jealous for it. They are coming to Jesus by the droves! They have become tired of the false and empty paths they have been traveling and are yearning for the genuine touch of God upon their lives.

God longs for us to discover the overwhelming sweetness and inexpressible pleasures of His presence. He wants all of us to enjoy and to live in the power of His Holy Spirit. He desires this so that we can hear His heartbeat for the salvation and release of many other captives. As it says in Song of Solomon 5:16, *"His mouth is most sweet: yes, he is altogether lovely. This is my beloved, and this is my friend, O daughters of Jerusalem!"* This love satisfies our souls and quiets us; it empowers and equips us. Only the fire of His passion can consume the old nature and transform us into His image. *"For our God is a consuming fire"* (Hebrews 12:29).

With renewed vision, many will hear His call to "do as He did." When commissioning His disciples, Jesus gave instructions that are no less true today: *"And these signs will follow those who will believe: In my name they will cast out demons; they will speak with new tongues;...they will lay hands on the sick, and they will recover"* (Mark 16:17-18). We are talking about real spiritual power here! May we, too, move fully into this anointing.

Although I continued to have some psychic experiences even after my conversion, they differed dramatically from the true spiritual experiences God was giving me. Over time, I was able to eliminate the false experiences through proper discernment and spiritual warfare—the chief "weapons" being the name of Jesus and the covering of His blood through worship and prayer. Daily abiding with the Lord gave me His peace and loving guidance.

TM COCKTAIL

After becoming a Christian, I quickly discovered that you cannot mix Christianity and TM. As already mentioned, I decided to try just one more session of TM "to see how things went." Soon after this meditation session, I had a very strange dream. In this dream I saw an entire football stadium filled with identical white statues seated in rows. Each statue resembled an idol with a pointed head, wearing the most garish red lipstick. When I contemplated this image, I felt a terrible unseen presence. The next day I had an "accident" while driving my car. After packing for an overnight trip, a suitcase fell off the top of my car, spilling the contents all over the road. I was able to retrieve everything that had been in the suitcase, all except the list of the TM mantras used during the initiation ceremonies. They were nowhere to be found. This was probably a sign from God.

As I grew in my understanding of the Christian faith, God revealed to me that even though Christians may attend different churches, there is really only one family of believers. The Holy Spirit led me to the church He wanted me to attend. One day during the church service the pastor asked for a show of hands of those who really needed God's help and direction. I raised my hand, feeling a little sheepish but knowing how badly I needed it. He said, "Vail, the Lord is telling me that there has been a very great hurt in your life." (My relationship with Sean had caused me great spiritual confusion and pain.) He said, "Jesus is going to pour out His Spirit upon your life and He's going to heal that hurt, but it will take some time." Later, in the middle of the night, I woke to a sense of joy and peace as the emotional healing began.

For a while I disciplined myself to sit down twice a day and pray and meditate on the Lord. After all, had I not given that much time to TM? One day the Holy Spirit wooed me and drew me closer to Himself, right in the middle of my activities. A sense of freedom and happiness on the inside continued to linger in the most restful and compelling way all day. God wants us to learn to abide in His presence even in activity. There is plenty of scriptural evidence that we do not ever have to leave this wonderful place of abiding, but it involves a process of continual choosing. We must know that He wants to inhabit the core of our being and be our point of reference, so we humbly defer to Him in all things. As we abide in Him, He will make our lives a glory and a wonder.

13

A Common Legacy

A YOGI FINDS JESUS

*J*ust before Sean departed with his band of followers, I had him post a note on the bulletin board of "Ma's Revolution," a local health food store. It was a request for anyone "into Jesus and raw foods" to contact me. The Lord supernaturally led a young man named Stanley to the announcement. He had just returned from walking up the Himalayan mountains and meditating on top of the pyramid of Giza in Egypt. As he was standing in the health food store reading the note, someone came up to him and asked, "Is your name Sean?" As Stanley noticed that the note was signed "Sean," he tuned into Sean's "vibes" and then immediately called me on the phone and came over. When he arrived at my apartment, he was wearing all white and carrying a big knapsack full of healing herbs and potions and some personal belongings, smelling wonderfully of essential oils.

Stanley and I shared a common legacy in many ways and became good friends. He had been initially introduced to the world of expanded awareness via marijuana and LSD, later winding up in the Haight-Ashbury district of San Francisco, possibly at the same time I was there. From the Haight, Stanley moved to Berkeley in 1968 just in time to observe the demonstrations, riots, barbed wire, and tear gas. We probably passed each other many times on the street without knowing it.

After exploring macrobiotics, hypnosis, Eastern religions, and meditation—indeed anything metaphysically oriented or connected with the psychic dimension—Stanley joined the Summit Lighthouse group in Colorado Springs under the leadership of Elizabeth Clare Prophet. The psychic and clairvoyant abilities that Stanley had discovered and developed enabled him to become the organization's "seer." He went much further than I did in his total dedication to becoming finely attuned psychically and spiritually to these other dimensions. Responding to what he thought was an invitation from the psychic realm to "Come and find me," he began seeking his hidden guru, by embarking barefoot on a 200-mile trek to the Himalayan mountain region with only a cloth wrapped around his waist and no hair on his head.

After picking off hundreds of leeches from his infected and depleted body and at a desperately low point in his journey, Stanley opened himself to the "Father" principle, crying out continually for God to reveal truth to him. While fervently praying for a revelation of truth, the Spirit of Jesus Christ appeared to him. Stanley was stunned finally to discover that the "Avatar" he had been searching for all these years was really the same Jesus he had only dimly perceived years before in Portland, Oregon, among a group of Jesus freaks.

Three days later on his knees, Stanley sought to confirm the vision of the exalted Christ, which he had perceived in his spirit. After praying to God for a confirmation, a giant rainbow appeared over the valley of the Himalayas that had not been there when he had begun his prayer only moments before. Inspired, he headed back for America.

DIVINE COINCIDENCE

It wasn't long after Stanley returned to the United States that he saw my note on the health food store bulletin board. Two days later the other Christian brothers in my apartment building joined me in praying for him. It was then that he experienced the Baptism in the Holy Spirit and a release from the oppression, which he later recognized as demonic activity. Simultaneously, God revealed to him that his former state of Eastern enlightenment ("samadhi") was really a spiritual counterfeit.

God immediately began to show Stanley how the true gifts of the Holy Spirit operate. He lived with Chris and David in a room down the hallway from mine. Each of these brothers were given different gifts of the Holy Spirit. It was like a fully operating church in microcosm. Once during the middle of the night in their sleep, Chris and David began to operate in the gifts of the Spirit. One of them spoke in tongues while the other one interpreted what the message in tongues meant. The interpreted message was meant for Stanley, who being awake at the time, was greatly edified!

I was also being taught simple lessons of faith. These brothers sometimes enjoyed playing loud music, and there was only a wall separating their room from mine. Once I could not sleep because of the loud music, but I didn't feel like getting up and going down the hallway to ask them to turn it down. I decided to ask Jesus to please have them turn off the music. Suddenly, everything was quiet. My friends had turned off their radio.

RENOUNCING OCCULTISM

Immediately upon receiving God's Holy Spirit, Stanley began a process of systematically replacing every one of his prior spiritual involvements with six months of prayer and Bible study in order for the Lord to strengthen him in the inner man and renew his mind. These are necessary steps for anyone who has been involved in deceptive spiritual and occult practices. (See the Appendix to this book for a testimonial tract that Stanley wrote.)

The Lord began to pour out his Spirit mightily upon Stanley, giving him the ability to teach and preach with healing gifts. He began to flow in other spiritual manifestations such as the gifts of the word of knowledge, the word of wisdom, and prophecy. God began to use him greatly. Stanley had given up his own psychic abilities, so God was willing to pour into that empty place his own *authentic* gifts of the Spirit.

THE WHITE PERIOD

Stanley and I still wore white, a remnant from Eastern mystical days. Although I had always worn regular clothes as a TM meditator, Sean and Stanley both convinced me to wear white because supposedly it had "higher vibes." One day while I was witnessing in front of the Student Union, a young Berkeley student seemed confused by the fact that I exuded the presence of Christ but was wearing white and beads like the yogis. I couldn't convince him that I was a true believer because he darted away to observe me from a "safe" distance. God used this "white" period in my life to help open up a few spiritual seekers to the Lord (but it drove away a few Christians!). It's not a bad idea to venture out of our comfortable church pews and identify with our lost world. If it takes a change in apparel, so be it. While still wearing white, Stanley and I were walking on the streets of Oakland one day when a man fell down at Stanley's feet, begging him to pray for him and asking God for mercy and forgiveness. We prayed for this man who was then saved and healed instantly of a serious physical condition. While the white clothes initially attracted this man, what really delivered him was the power of God. Stanley often prayed and scripturally meditated many hours a day, studying God's Word and discovering its rich jewels of life-giving knowledge.

NARROW ESCAPES

Soon after Stanley's conversion, he discovered that the young daughter of a close family friend was engaged to be married to a Mormon. This man was old enough to be her father, and he already had one wife. With several others from our church, Stanley, my brother Ed, and I piled into a station wagon and headed to Salt Lake City to rescue this young girl named Linda. Ed had not yet made a commitment to Christ; he came along for human-interest reasons. He is a photographer, so he caught a lot of interesting pictures of our journey.

We drove for a long time and arrived in Salt Lake City at 4:00 A.M. First, we spent time with Linda's family. The mother repented of several things in her life, and the entire family prayed to receive Jesus as Lord! Linda's sister invited her boyfriend over and after presenting the Gospel to him and praying, he became filled with the Holy Spirit. His body literally shook for an hour afterwards. Such an experience is how the Quakers originally got their name.

The Lord had a wonderful snow come down out of season—three feet of it. I think He did it just to please Bill, one of the brothers who had come with us from Berkeley. He had never seen snow before and had never been outside of California. Bill was so excited to see the snow that he went outside and *ate* some of it. Meanwhile, I was upstairs reading some scriptures and praying, and when Bill came inside I read it to him, unaware that Bill had been eating the snow. God has an interesting way of showing up sometimes!

> *For as the rain comes down, and the **snow** from heaven, and do not return there, but water the earth, and make it bring forth and bud, that it may give seed to the sower and bread to the eater: so shall My word be that goes forth from my mouth; it shall not return to Me void, but it shall accomplish what I please, and it shall prosper in the thing for which I sent it.*

> (Isaiah 55:10-11)

The next day Linda called her Mormon fiancé and asked him if some friends of hers could speak briefly with the head of the Mormon Church in his office. (This man had eight wives and was considered very spiritual.) We waited in the lobby praying fervently under our breath, while Stanley paced back and forth holding a huge "Bible thumper" edition in his hands. When the head elder invited us into his office, Stanley was in austere prophetic form. Everyone has their own style. I'm not saying this is how I would have done it, but maybe the man needed the frontal approach. Stanley threw his Bible down on the man's desk, opened to a key passage that deals with the sin of adultery, and told him in no uncertain terms that he needed to repent. He declared that the Mormon doctrine is not of God and shared a few other things. Red faced and trembling with rage, the elder kicked all of us out and said he didn't want to go to our kind of heaven.

We witnessed to Linda's Mormon friend who was by now her ex-fiancé. We encountered heavy spiritual opposition in sharing the truth with him. The spirit behind the man was cunning, and the man was a real subtle, psychological manipulator who didn't want to accept the evidence. After this encounter we left with Linda and her sister for California where they received counseling in the faith until their return to Utah.

On our way back from Salt Lake City we took an exciting trip down the coast to Southern California to visit Stanley's former affiliation, the Summit Lighthouse. During a break between classes we began to pass out our material. Many of the students were walking around outside the building acting hostile, and only a few of them took our literature. Some of them were touched by our message but were afraid to show it. We were all told to leave, and as we stood on the sidewalk, a friend of Hal Lindsay, who wrote _The Late Great Planet Earth,_ drove up and asked us what we were doing. We felt this was a sign to us that the Lord was totally with us.

While witnessing to these Summit Lighthouse people, Stanley asked me if I noticed a purplish sticky energy coming at us. He said they were trying to bombard us with mantras and psychic energy. I had noticed it, so we rebuked the spirits in Jesus' name and authority and prayed for Mrs. Prophet and the others. (Later, during another trip to the Summit Lighthouse, Stanley was able to speak directly with Mrs. Prophet. She became angry and would not listen to him. But seeds of eventual deliverance had been planted in many hearts.) One Canadian fellow stepped outside the fence and came back with us to Berkeley. He experienced a mighty deliverance and the power of the Holy Spirit at one of the church services.

I prayed for God to do something for my brother on this journey. The Lord had promised me that before we returned home, Ed would find Christ. As it later turned out, we were only five minutes outside of Oakland on our return trip. I had almost entirely forgotten God's promise about my brother, when the power of the Holy Spirit came upon our group. Stanley, unaware of the Lord's promise to me, suddenly began to prophesy to Ed about his need to receive Jesus as Lord. Stanley led Ed in the prayer of salvation, and then everyone began to say that they sensed angels rejoicing all around the car. My brother wound up finding more than a human adventure—he received the Source of eternal life.

14

Resurrection City
Center For Authentic Enlightenment

*I*n January, 1975, Stanley, another friend, and I formed a ministry called "The Center for Authentic Enlightenment" located in the Resurrection City Church building under the leadership of Mario Murillo. We primarily studied and compared Christianity with other spiritual paths, offering ourselves as speakers and teachers to those seeking to understand the uniqueness of Christianity. We had many opportunities to present the true Christ to individuals and groups in the San Francisco Bay area. At this time I began to experience a mighty outpouring of God's Spirit. As people came up to us after our talks, we would pray for them. We saw many conversions and powerful deliverances from evil spirits.

Stanley was a great person to work with, and he was able to spiritually discern my occasional lapses in good judgment. Once I was walking by the Hare Krishna group near the campus while they were serving their meal out on the lawn. After tasting a few of their goodies, I decided I would like to learn some of their delicious recipes. I went to the bookstore, bought a Hare Krishna cookbook, and took it home to my apartment. Soon Stanley came in and said that while he was walking along he had heard the words, "Hare Krishna, Hare Krishna." He followed the sound up the street and right into my apartment. He asked me what in the world I had been doing. It seems that keeping literature from an occult organization in your home can attract "unwanted spiritual entities." So I sacrificed the cookbook, but memorized how to make sticky balls. After all, a sticky ball is just a sticky ball.

SCHOOL OF THE SPIRIT
A Pact With God

One day Stanley gave me a prophecy that God would be bringing me through His "School of the Spirit." He also said that God would someday open up to me opportunities to speak all over the country about TM and the occult, and that he would also be bringing to pass a ministry involving a book. (Here it is.) But there was one small thing in my life God wanted me to lay down sacrificially. He said that God would eventually have his way in my life and give me victory in this matter. It may not seem very important but it was to me, because it involved my self-image. It was important to God though, because the Bible says that if we cannot obey Him in the little things, how can He entrust us with more? Furthermore, obedience and faithfulness in the small matters proves us worthy to handle more, so it was a test. My prayer is that this little episode will help my readers to have the courage to trust Jesus in all things. He is the God of "tough love." He gets down to our real motives.

The Lord was asking me to give up my facial exercises. What He requires from one person is not the same as for someone else. Everyone told me I looked young for my age, and I wanted to keep it that way. I had read a book describing how certain facial exercises can keep the muscles of a person's face firm well up into their eighties. I saw nothing wrong with doing this; after all, who wants to look like a prune if they don't have to? I had been diligently doing these facial exercises fifteen minutes a day for several years. One day in front of the mirror God revealed to me that He wanted me to give them up. He said that Jesus would not be doing facial exercises, that they were time consuming, self-centered, and that _in my life_ they were like an idol. Furthermore, He pointed out that older women would be able to relate to me even better if I looked more like them. (I did not like that idea at all!) Then He asked me a hard question: "Which is more important to you, loving others or loving yourself?" O.K., now we're getting down to the nitty gritty.

Around this time Stanley, not knowing about my inner conflict, gave me a book to read entitled, _Rees Howells, Intercessor_. It was all about a man called by God to intercede for an Allied victory in World War II. An important requirement was Reese Howells' being willing to give up his favorite hat that he wore at all times. For some reason his identity was so tied up with wearing this hat that he felt utterly humiliated, naked, and foolish when he was not wearing it. But God put His finger on that hat and told Reese that he must give up wearing it. After a painful struggle he finally relinquished his hat, and because of that small sacrifice (which to him was HUGE), God greatly blessed him with powerful intercessions that helped defeat Hitler's armies. What God asks a person to do might seem small, but you never know what impact it will bring.

Probably every one of us has some sort of identity tag, which we feel we cannot live without. For some it might be aspiring to make the football team. For a musician friend of mine, it was his guitar. The Lord told him to sacrifice it (for a season), but he felt it was too costly and just could not bring himself to do it. As a result he did not have the spiritual power to stay in the faith and eventually drifted away. God told another brother to give up his guitar as well, and he did. Later on the Lord gave him back his guitar and blessed him musically more than before. The Lord had to prune him so he could be more fruitful.

In becoming a follower of Jesus, it can be tough when He requires something of us that we don't want to release to Him. If we do not obey in these little matters, we will always be carrying around inside of us that "what if?" feeling. I know I would dread facing Jesus someday about it. The Bible says that "...*whatsoever is not of faith is sin*" (Romans 14:23 KJV). He just wants to be first in everything we do, and then He will give us more. The Lord does not enjoy withholding things from us and is not stingy. But if the truth be known, many will not come to Christ because they want a God who is far off and not one who will mess with their personal issues.

I felt that if I suddenly quit doing my facial exercises, I might turn into a time-warp facsimile of the very old woman in the movie, "Shangri-la." (The minute she stepped outside the sheltered mountain atmosphere where she had always lived, she turned into a mass of horrible wrinkles.) One of my problems has been an overactive imagination. I'm sorry to confess it took me about three years to finally give up the facial exercises. The Lord just kept dealing with me about it. In the car one day Stanley, who was unaware of all this, said that the Holy Spirit had given him some words for me: "If you will give Me your youth, I will give you Mine." Also, a newly-saved, Spirit-filled teenage girl I knew suddenly looked at me with a big grin, and with no prior knowledge of my situation said, "Be ugly for Jesus." I got terribly convicted.

God's pressure has a way of increasing when we don't immediately obey. I'm sure God wanted to pull out of me the root of self-centeredness and fear of aging. The hippies, baby boomers, Gen-X'ers, and anyone who has been a willing victim of the youth-cult advertising industry, all dread getting older and losing their youth. Many of them already have! Some of them have managed to patch the leak in the dyke with plastic surgery, special diets, and fetishes of one kind or another. I went into one of the office rooms at our church and saw a picture of Jesus on the wall in the pose of Uncle Sam with his finger pointing straight at me. The caption read, "This is absolutely your last chance to obey Me on this matter!"

BEAUTY FOR ASHES

That did it! God finally had His way. I went into one of the back prayer rooms and knelt weeping and gave Jesus my facial exercises. When I came out, I sat down and started playing the piano. Suddenly it seemed out of nowhere several young girls ran to the piano and gathered around it. As we sang together, I was dazzled by joy as I heard and felt angels all around us rejoicing and praising God. Obedience to God in even the very small matters can open the door to new blessings and new beginnings. At the piano with these lovely worshippers, I felt an anointing resting upon me for something concerning a future ministry to the youth. Years later I began doing black-light chalk art presentations involving music, special lights, and fluorescent chalk, to give these young "instant messengers" dramatic life-like presentations from the teachings of Jesus in a format designed especially for them.

It has been years since this incident. God has been faithful to me in everything small or large. Though I no longer do facial exercises, I have enjoyed the benefits of looking and feeling much younger than my years. God was true to His promise that if I would give Him my youth, He would give me His.

BOOK OF REVELATION

The Scriptures speak of a time of great distress upon all nations, and it is called the Great Tribulation. It certainly is described in detail in the last book of the Bible. Many books and movies have been made about it. Most religions attest to it in some way. God revealed to me that this time of the end was not very far away and that I must prepare for it.

One night as I was sleeping in my apartment at the ministry house, a most extraordinary thing occurred. A group of us had been having an impromptu Bible study on the book of *Revelation* about the end times and the Antichrist. After I went to bed, I dreamed that I was sleeping in an upper room full of other believers. As the dream unfolded, I awoke to the footsteps of what seemed like a thief coming up the back stairs of the house. As the steps grew closer, I started to feel terrified and unprepared. The Bible speaks of Jesus coming to the earth like a thief, only to find many Christians spiritually asleep like those in my dream. The parable of the ten virgins came to mind. Five of them had their lamps trimmed with oil and were ready and waiting for the Bridegroom to come; the other five were not ready and were *shut out* from the marriage feast (Matthew 25:1-13).

Now fully alert, I could hear the footsteps reaching the top of the stairs. Suddenly my eyes were drawn to a picture on the wall of Jesus standing in a field filled with many flowers, trees, and birds. He was holding a lamb in

His arms. The street light shining through my window shade seemed to laser-light Jesus' face with white-hot intensity. Shadows from the trees outside cast a form on my window shade of a man wearing dark glasses and a crown on his head, obviously some kind of an earthly king or political leader. Out of his mouth were jumping three frogs. The book of *Revelation* paints a similar picture: *"And I saw three unclean spirits like frogs coming out of the mouth of the dragon, out of the mouth of the beast, and out of the mouth of the false prophet"* (Revelation 16:13).

THE BRIDE OF CHRIST

As the vision continued, I saw a huge bouquet of flowers. The air was filled with an unearthly and sweet fragrance, and there stood the beautiful bride of Christ in all her glory. The bouquet was not quite ready, but she was being prepared. I could see that the Bride will be composed of two groups of Christians in the last days. Some will be prepared, and some will have neglected this most important matter. But the heart of the Lord Jesus Christ is yearning for a special bride who will be wearing a garment of pure white linen, holy and spotless. Her eyes will look steadfastly upon only Him, and nothing in this world will be able to take His place in her heart. She will not be distracted by the worries and cares of life, no matter how pressing. Her only desire will be to please Him. And she will not be spiritually asleep so as to miss His arrival.

When this extraordinary vision was over, there was a knock on the door. Stanley and a girl named Kit came in. Stanley said to me, "Vail, your face is shining with the glory of God, like Moses! What happened?" I told them about the vision the Lord had just given me, but I was so overcome I could hardly stand up or speak. Another girl came into the room and when I told her what I had seen, she fell to her knees weeping. She kept saying, "I don't know why I am crying." The power of God was so strong in the room, much greater than my experience of the infilling of the Holy Spirit. It was so strong that it seemed to "burn" within my whole being. There was a sense of His holiness that caused an immediate sense of my total imperfection before God. I understood the scripture that says:

> *But who can endure the day of His coming? And who can stand when He appears? For He is like a refiner's fire and like launderers' soap. He will sit as a refiner and a purifier of silver; He will purify the sons of Levi, and purge them as gold and silver, that they may offer to the LORD an offering in righteousness.*
>
> (Malachi 3:2-3)

We should seek to know Him in His glory. God is like a tender mother in his love for us, but at the same time He is majestic, powerful, and full of authority. No one can experience His awesome glory and remain unchanged. I don't think I will ever take God for granted or regard him casually after having had this experience.

EQUAL TIME

Attending Mario Murillo's church and being on staff "stretched" me and was very rewarding. Meanwhile I took up the daily challenge of giving myself more and more to serving others and trying to live a life of true discipleship. Since Mario moved in such a mighty way in the gifts of the Spirit, our staff meetings were never boring. At one particular meeting Mario said that the Lord was going to be setting me free from "easy believism." My life as a Christian was to go through many years of the dealings of God in order to surrender more fully to his will. It is not easy to switch from believing all ways are pleasing to God, to walking out absolute obedience and death to self-will on the "narrow way" of the cross. Jesus spoke of the "broad way" that leads to death versus the "narrow way" that leads to eternal life (Matthew 7:13). Also, Scripture says _"There is a way that seems right to a man, but its end is the way of death"_ (Proverbs 14:12). Obviously this is an important life and death issue. Which way will you choose?

In the Spring a Logan High School Christian student, Nancy, persuaded her teacher to invite Stanley to give a three-day seminar in a class called "Tripping," the most popular class in the school (naturally)! I went along to assist him. During the school year the line-up of illustrious speakers had included witches, warlocks, psychics, satanists, and astrologers. Stanley's seminar was the last one of the season, and he had been preceded by a Baha'i faith speaker. After three days the teacher confessed to being in a witches coven, was delivered of at least three demons, and six students received Christ. At the end of the class the biggest joker in the school came up to us with a swollen little finger and asked us to pray for it to see if the Lord could heal as Stanley had claimed. He and I prayed over the boy's finger and watched the swelling go down. Pain free, the young man walked away amazed. Before we left, we invited the students to come to a crusade led by Mario Murillo.

The night of the crusade, Mario gave the altar call and then the Spirit of God began supernaturally to move over the audience with many spontaneous healings. Those responding received prayer and counseling. I was one of the counselors, and when I returned to the auditorium, I went and sat beside a girl named Nancy near the back. I was startled when Mario suddenly called out, "Vail, pray for the person near you who is being healed of a lung condition. His left lung is being cleared." I did not know who the person might be, but a guy standing behind Nancy said, "I think it's me." So I extended my hand and prayed that the Lord would totally heal him, all the while experiencing a Divine presence behind me. Out of the huge crowd of people there, this young man was a student from the class Stanley had been teaching. He was totally healed! It was the Lord's way of having Logan High School convinced beyond a doubt of the authenticity of the Scriptures.

At another high school a TM teacher had been invited to speak to the psychology class. Some parents demanded "equal time" and asked that I be given the opportunity to counter the TM position, so they invited me to be the speaker. When I arrived at the psychology class, I just pulled up a chair and sat informally in front of the students, who were very quiet and attentive. After my talk a few girls came up to me and said that they "felt different" and wanted to speak with me privately. We went outside and sat on the lawn, and there they prayed to receive the Lord Jesus into their hearts. In a quiet way their lives had been changed forever.

After hearing my presentation at the New Life Ministry at Chabot College, the English teacher (who had been recommending TM to his class) asked me to present the other side of the story to his students. During the talk I felt the power of God at work, and I noticed that the teacher was visibly agitated. Red faced, he began pounding his desk and declaring that TM is a way to God and that we must "realize" God within us. The entire class could see that he had no real peace. His actions spoke volumes to them.

CHALLENGING OPPORTUNITIES

Doors started opening for me to speak about TM on television and radio. The late Dr. Walter Martin's study group on the cults sent someone to interview me for their regular Saturday radio show. Also, a reporter and camera man from Channel 11 in Los Angeles interviewed me at the airport. He asked me simple questions about why I quit TM. I explained what I felt were some serious deceptions in TM and described my experience with near-possession. I also witnessed about the amazing change Jesus had brought in my life.

One of my most challenging opportunities was the invitation to debate a TM instructor on the 6:00 P.M. news in Eugene, Oregon. The TM instructor came with all his "Goliath" notes and responses memorized. I came with my slingshot of personal experience, prayer, and faith. I believed firmly that God would give me the wisdom I needed to truthfully and forcefully present the case against TM.

Sitting in the filming area, I felt the anointing of God's peace. The TM instructor seemed organized and sure of himself. However, he began to look nervous as he saw my total lack of stress or fear. When you are resting in the truth, nothing can shake you. Perhaps he expected someone more edgy and hysterical since the TM organization had undoubtedly blamed my leaving TM on an enormous case of "unstressing." Even though I had not memorized my notes, I spoke the truth clearly. Many months later I had the pleasure of encountering some young girls on the University of Colorado campus who had seen this TV debate in Oregon and had prayed for me. They had also asked God to let them meet me someday.

CATHOLIC CONVENT RETREAT

After learning that a Catholic Convent was offering a retreat in the countryside with a special emphasis on silent meditation, I decided to attend it. We weren't supposed to talk for three days and spent much time in solitary prayer and devotions. At the end of the time we all came together and discussed what it meant to us. While I was there, it came to my attention that many nuns and participants were practicing TM. When the discussion time came around, I stood and announced that I was a former teacher of Transcendental Meditation, that TM is a religion (stemming from Hinduism), and that the mantras given for repetition were the names of false gods or fallen spirits forbidden by Scriptures to serious believers. That stirred up quite a controversy, but the overseeing priest commended me and said that I had been sent by God, and for everyone to consider carefully what I shared.

BOULDER CAMPUS

The Lord graciously opened many other doors for my testimony, such as Aglow International meetings all over the San Francisco Bay area. One invitation brought me to the University of Colorado at Boulder where the Cult Awareness Ministry had blitzed the campus with posters that bore the words, "Is TM a Religion?" Speaking in the very room where TM teachers gave their weekly lectures, I answered many questions and explained TM's deception to a large audience. A write-up on my talk appeared the following day in the campus newspaper. Exposing TM wasn't my idea of a fun thing to do, but I felt it was necessary for the sake of honesty and truth. Somebody had to do it.

In the dining room of the Student Union a young man who had been at my talk warned me that he thought what I was doing seemed dangerous and that I should be careful. I thanked him for his concern but assured him that anyone who would try to cause me trouble would have to get permission from my Master first. Since it was His mission, He would provide me with everything I needed, including divine "body guards" (huge, powerful angels—I've seen them). He hasn't failed me yet.

ARGUMENTS OF LUNATICS

While in Boulder, I was looking forward to a talk I was to give in a local church. It was expected that several TM teachers would attend. We prayerfully placed some clearly written material on a stand in the lobby. When I saw the teachers come in and sit together near the back, I asked God to reveal Himself to them. It was a special opportunity to show them the love and compassion of Jesus Christ. I fervently longed for them to find the truth and the kind of freedom that only Christ can give.

In my talk I told everyone that Christians must witness to those in TM with love and not condemnation. Following the presentation, a TM teacher got up and said he felt I had misrepresented TM. He gave his credentials—a baptized Methodist, father of two, practiced TM for eight years—when suddenly some unstable man jumped up from the audience and pointed at him, saying, "You are Satan! You are Satan!" The whole place was in an uproar. The TM teacher turned white as a sheet and ran out of the church, and I didn't blame him. On his heels was this crazy man yelling, "I cast you out of my Father's house!" After a few minutes the four or five other TM teachers sitting in the back made a hasty retreat, leaving our literature on the pews. After all, why should they read the arguments of lunatics? Undoubtedly, their worst suspicions about born-again believers were reinforced that day.

This reaction, of course, is an example of HOW NOT TO RELATE to those who don't know Christ, especially those from a subtle, quiet discipline such as Eastern meditation. All I could do was pray that they would be able to overlook this extreme case of hate and hysteria. I have always wanted personally to say to those TM teachers, "I'm really sorry that we offended you. Please forgive us. There's a weird one in every bunch." For any others who have experienced a lack of kindness or sensitivity from uninformed Christians, my apologies go to you as well. Don't dismiss the message of salvation because of people who are not acting as they should.

Many Christians do understand where people involved with TM are coming from. God is the Lord of quiet rest and deep fulfillment, but He uses imperfect, yet unfinished human vessels to present His message. Sometimes Christians try to speak out about spiritual things beyond their present level of spiritual maturity, so please be patient with them. To even the score, I knew just as many strange people among TM meditators, especially the TM initiators. The difference is their destiny.

THINGS REALLY HEAT UP

I surprised some of my TM teacher friends by showing up at a presentation they were giving to parents of students at the Berkeley campus. They were trying to convince them of all the benefits of TM and why it should be taught at the university. The teachers, unaware that I had left TM, thought nothing of my appearance. When it was time for questions and answers, however, I stood up and identified myself as a "former TM teacher." Then I proceeded to expose TM's hidden agenda and to identify it as a form of Hinduism, having no place in the schools. This was not easy! The situation really heated up, and for me it was accentuated by the tablespoon of cayenne pepper I had taken in a glass of water earlier that day as a new experimental health regimen. (My entire alimentary canal was on fire!) Through this trial by fire, I believe that many college students were spared from TM's deception.

HINDUISM BY ANY OTHER NAME...

When TM came in like a flood to deceive both ordinary citizens and students, the Spirit of God really raised a standard. I was working for the Spiritual Counterfeits Project part-time. One of the things I did was to present their slide show to various groups of people in the San Francisco Bay area. A fellow Christian named David Haddon approached me one day and told me that Baker Book House Publishers wanted us to co-author a book about Transcendental Meditation from a Christian perspective. So we wrote a book entitled _TM Wants You,_ now out of print. In this book I gave the whole inside scoop about TM—the deceptions, lying, incongruities, and what exactly goes on during the initiation process. The mantras were revealed to be the names of Hindu deities (demon-gods), and the religious nature of the practice was made clear.

Hindu writers themselves admit that a non-Hindu who meditates or calls on the name of a deity unknowingly is nevertheless practicing Hinduism. The presence of the spirits causes the unsuspecting meditator to be pulled psychically into a non-Biblical experience and world view.

David and I joined some members of the Spiritual Counterfeits Project (SCP) in attending a political cocktail party so that we could inform Assemblyman Ken Meade about the fact that TM is a religion, not a science. Ken was running for office and wanted to introduce TM into the school systems in the Bay Area. When I told him that, contrary to the 'scientific' claims, TM is a religious technique, he was amazed. A meditator himself, he was unaware of the deeper religious teachings. I also pointed out that TM does not necessarily increase one's creativity as advertised. He was shocked and disappointed, but could not deny my arguments. The Christians from SCP were pleased and surprised at the fearless boldness they saw coming from me. It was Jesus and His enabling that made me bold. I really don't come by it naturally.

BLISSED OUT WHILE ROME BURNS

An article in *Psychology Today* (July 1975, p. 50) reported on experiments that revealed that creative people generate more alpha waves when they are creative and fewer when they are resting. Normal or noncreative people, on the other hand, register fewer alpha waves when involved in tasks that require creative effort, and more when they rest. The parallel study on creativity revealed that TM teachers scored the same as or worse than the "normal or noncreative" control groups.[12] The inference was that the huge amount of alpha waves generated during meditations may make one feel rewarded without ever doing anything creative to deserve it; hence, they are feasting at the banquet of psychic pleasures "while Rome burns."

The article stated further that creative people normally have many fluctuations in their skin conductance. The altered state of consciousness produced by TM makes one's skin less conductive, giving one the experience of peace without effort or contribution. Is there a high price to be paid for this calmness? The price may very well be a kind of dangerous passivity and isolation.

A DEEPER CHRIST-LIKENESS

While collaborating with David on our book, I met a woman named Lillian who was writing a book on Christian meditation. She and I taught several classes on how to meditate Biblically. I emphasized that Christian meditation is not so much for us—it is for the Lord to have His way in us. Selfish motives need to be confessed and removed. Of course, we do benefit. It is God's desire that we achieve our full potential, but it can only happen as we yield ourselves to Him, holding nothing back.

I am sure that most spiritual seekers have questions that arise within their hearts—questions they would like to have answered. Jesus can answer every question we have and enlighten us when we seek to be spiritually united with Him. Without God we cannot recognize the truth; we may be filled with erroneous thoughts, which come from our human nature. The Adversary knows how to mislead us into self-love. That is why it is so important to follow the guidance of the inspired Scriptures; otherwise one can fall into the error of desiring to achieve blissfulness for selfish motives. Great deliverance comes from placing the commandments higher than our own desires. It is important to pay attention to Biblical warnings that grant us the wisdom to make wise choices. This determines our future.

Following the lie (self-exaltation of the fallen nature) is what originally brought death, instead of life, into the world.

Unfortunately, Biblical meditation is often misunderstood and omitted from the lives of many Christians who don't realize the enrichment it brings! God gave me authentic Biblical meditation to replace the counterfeit. After a couple of years of practicing Christian meditation, I was led by the Holy Spirit to center more on worship and intercession. But I believe that most people need to include more "listening prayer" and "silent meditation" (soaking in His Presence) in their time of worship. Focusing on the person of Jesus, divinely inspired truths, and His wonderful name opens us to His love and guidance and power. We should ask Jesus to bring us to the Father, and for the Father's love to minister to us. This will produce in us a deeper Christ-likeness and "sonship" that attracts others. Superficial Christianity will not change us, and it certainly will not change anyone else. It is one thing to be born again and to study God's Word, but we must be willing to "walk the talk." Jesus didn't come to this earth to die an agonizing death so that we could warm Sunday church pews. Jesus came to be the firstborn of a new order of beings: sons of God (His "brethren") who will be *like Him,* doing His works and greater.

BOOKS AND FILM

At this time in my life Jeremiah Films contacted me about giving my testimony in a movie called "Cult Explosion." Several authors included me in their books. These included a book by Rabi Maharaj, *The Meditators* by Douglas Shah, *The Transcendental Explosion* by John

Weldon with Zola Levitt, and some others. I have had the privilege of touching many lives through my testimony.

Of special interest is the co-founder of Jeremiah Films whose name is Caryl Matrisciana. She appears in the film, _Gods of the New Age_—a documentation of the rise of Hinduism in the West. The yoga she saw when she lived in India was, as she put it, "intense, arduous, and serious—a discipline taught by avowed spiritual masters who prepared their disciples for death!" It was anything but the popular, sweet, exciting new spiritual experience embraced by yoga practitioners and hippies in the West. Caryl had always seen reincarnation as a "terrible prison with no escape," and yet even she yielded to the pressure to embrace the New Age and debunk the Christian faith, until her conversion. Her films and videos give invaluable insights from a well-informed insider familiar with both traditions and knowing their vast difference.

MALNAK VERSUS YOGI

In an effort to stop TM from being taught in the schools, SCP (Spiritual Counterfeits Project) took the TM movement to court (_Malnak versus Yogi_, 1973). The judge ruled that TM was a form of Hinduism and could no longer be taught in public schools because it violated the separation of church and state. I was one of the key witnesses in this court case. Maharishi felt TM's setback was due to the malevolent actions of a very powerful demon that was determined to retard the spiritual growth of human beings.

Many students across the country are very grateful that they did not waste their resources or their lives on TM. However, the issue is still alive, as thirty years later the TM organization is still trying to get TM into the schools and to promote Maharishi's global agenda. Some public schools have managed to avoid the church-state separation issue by providing TM through private funding and off-hour meditations and instruction. As always, it is important to be aware of what is happening behind the scenes in the education of our children.

15

Global Transformation

THE WINDS SHIFT

*A*fter so much direct interaction with those in the New Age, I began to realize that God was changing His emphasis in my life. His goal was to bring about spiritual growth and maturity. So I began to receive several important words from various people concerning some new directions for my life.

A beloved elder in our church who had a revelatory gift, spoke to me of two books in my life. On one book was written, "The testimony you've been giving in the Bay Area is for people to recognize the Spirit of God and truth operating in your life. There is a real test now of the Word of God in your life" (the second book.) "Do not be overcome with perfectionism, but enjoy the process as God leads you into greater understanding." The Scriptures tell us that He must increase, but we (self) must decrease (John 3:30).

Through other prophecies I was warned that I would be experiencing a very strong pull from the world and that I needed to strengthen myself with a deeper understanding of the Scriptures. As I look back, I realize that Christians I knew who only relied on their experiences and their emotions without the important essential input of daily Bible study and prayer invariably fell back into deception.

A visiting prophet to our church, Dick Mills, said that the Lord would be confirming and revealing His leading concerning my life and ministry through nightly visions and dreams. He said, "If anyone insists on you doing something, just tell them you'll sleep on it." I have experienced many dreams and visions over the years and have received much valuable information from God this way. In 2002 I began to receive training under John Paul Jackson's Streams Ministries, and have become a certified dream interpreter. Streams Ministries encourages dream teams to go into the streets and marketplaces: coffee shops, malls, bookstores, or wherever there is an opportunity to give free dream interpretations. It is a lot of fun and very effective. This kind of dream interpretation is not to be confused with the New Age versions that can be found on the internet and other places.

In March 1975 Mario Murillo took me aside and told me that because of the call of God on my life, He had not allowed any man to "see" me as his wife. But that time was coming to a close, as the Lord was bringing me a husband, and for me to start preparing my heart. I began to seek the Lord about this, and in June the Lord confirmed this to me. He said simply: "You'll be getting married soon." The Lord's concept of "soon," however, is usually much different from ours. One day on my knees weeping, I asked Jesus if it was too hard a thing for him to search all his sons and bring me the right one? The Holy Spirit said, *"Be delayed and wait"* (Isaiah 29:9, NASB). Naturally, I was concerned about being able to have children. After attending a wedding and seeing one of my few remaining single friends married, I went through what was now becoming a ritual. I would kneel by my bed, cry, and pray. Following one of those episodes, God made me realize that if I were to find a husband, it would not be in the church I was attending at that time.

I am convinced that those who will trust God and truly die to their rights to be married, even facing the real possibility that they will never be married—a formidable thought for most of us—to these He will give His very best.

WHO IS THIS MAN?

After I began to work at the Spiritual Counterfeits Project as a typist, a man named Joe Carruth moved to Berkeley from Arkansas and took a job at SCP. Although he started out as mail clerk, his real love was writing, and some of his articles came out in the _SCP Journal_. It is ironic that I almost missed my divine appointment to meet Joe. I had made plans to move. The day before I was to leave, a friend who always had encouraged me to consider moving north, suddenly changed his mind. My disbelieving ears heard him say, "If you do move, you may never know what you missed." One week later I met Joe and a new chapter began to unfold in our lives. How a lifetime can turn on one decision!

I found that Joe had been a TM meditator like me. Because we had this in common, SCP asked the two of us to counsel a group of former TM teachers in Arizona. I wasn't surprised when SCP sent us. I had already received a vivid dream that Joe and I were sitting together in an airplane headed for Arizona. The Lord used us in the lives of three couples. Two couples came completely out of TM and joined a fellowship of believers; the third couple severed their relationship because the man would not tolerate his wife's Christianity. The Bible says, _"Can two walk together, unless they are agreed?"_ (Amos 3:3).

We frequently reached out to those in the New Age spirituality and gave the SCP slide show wherever it was needed. We both had a heart for those caught in TM and for street people, hippies, and fringe Christians. We enjoyed being friends with them. One day at the laundromat, I ran into a woman named Delores. She was always trying to get people to come with her on a "missionary" boat trip to China, and Joe was first on her list. She did not believe that Jesus ever suffered. When I showed her where Jesus said He would have to suffer and die, she started screaming with rage. I had upset her apple cart, but I had fun asking Joe when he was going to go to China.

I invited a nominal Christian street-hippie named Jeff to a meeting where Mario was preaching. Even though Jeff claimed to follow Jesus, he had never seemed to grasp what Jesus could do for him. He still wore a marble, occult charm around his neck "for good luck." I gently suggested he might pray about removing it and trusting Jesus instead. There was a strong presence of Jesus in the church meeting that evening. Mario preached against idolatry and double-mindedness. In the middle of his sermon I suddenly heard a loud cracking noise. Turning my head, I noticed that Jeff had gotten off the pew and was fumbling around on the floor trying to locate the other half of the charm. It had split right down the center! This talisman was made of a solid marble material, not likely to suddenly crack and fall apart. I asked Jeff if God was trying to tell him something, but he remained visibly unaffected. That incident reminded me of the Old Testament account of how God supernaturally destroyed an altar of idol worship (1 Kings 13:1-6).

WHOLE EARTH FESTIVAL

Living in Berkeley was quite exciting and challenging. Now that I was a full-fledged believer, I never lacked an opportunity to tell people about Jesus. Once I attended the annual Whole Earth Festival in Davis, California, where scores of spiritual groups had put up booths and exhibits. There were only two Christian groups there—SCP and a Catholic charismatic group. The Catholic group had set up a tent and communion table on the lawn. They invited people to take the sacraments and prayed for them with the laying on of hands. Through their prayer the power of God was manifested and sent many of them to the lawn, one by one. (This is called being "slain in the Spirit.")

The reaction of those from the mystical groups around us was interesting. They derided these experiences as "cheap" and "disgusting." From their point of view, the Christians were being "emotional" or faking it. None of them wanted to learn whether this demonstration of God's power was genuine. Although these criticisms stemmed from a gross lack of understanding, it was sad to see their ridicule and closed-mindedness. The following year it seemed to be more difficult for Christians to obtain a permit for an exhibit booth.

During my time at the festival I met a man who the Spirit of God revealed was high on some hallucinogen, probably LSD. I told him that I knew he was tripping. Then I began to present the message of salvation to him. Under my breath I was silently praying and binding the forces of darkness that were controlling him. I did not give up even when he seemed too stoned to listen. Another Christian, whom I did not know, stood behind me, supporting my efforts by praying and interceding for this man's soul. Miraculously the man slowly became responsive and was able to hear the plan of redemption with some interest. It usually takes a much longer time to come down from the influence of hallucinogens. Prayer is so powerful.

ADAPT OR PERISH?

When I saw an advertisement for a seminar given by the Wholistic Health and Nutrition Institute on "Slowing Down The Aging Process," I decided to attend. I should have come with a friend because Jesus advised His disciples to go in pairs. As well as learning about diet, exercise and enhancing the living process, I observed some unusual, hidden strategies at work. Most of the seminar was either technical data for nurses and doctors or general information about aging for the rest of the audience.

The last lecture given by Peter Keagan summed up the thrust of the seminar. His talk included slides of integrated holistic habitats for survival—homes and living communities that recycle heat, waste, and water, including the use of solar energy. Another topic covered greenhouses that can grow food at phenomenal rates to feed large populations. Keagan called these habitats, "Well-being Centers for Healing and Learning." He advocated an "Earthian Service Academy" to train people to work in these centers. Throughout his presentation pictures of Maharishi flashed subliminally on the screen behind him. He sounded a lot like Maharishi, using phrases such as "It's so easy, so effortless." Halfway through his talk, a slide was projected on the screen with a huge title in black letters, NOVUS ORDO SECLORUM, New Order of the Ages. Then a picture appeared from *Psychology Today* depicting meditators from all walks of life with a pyramid and "all-seeing eye" behind them. Over the pyramid was the same motto, "Novus Ordo Seclorum." Keagan intoned: "Stress, tension, aging—that's what's killing us," cryptically adding this troubling statement: "Those who adapt will survive. Those who do not adapt will not survive."

Could there come a time in the future when there will be a new discrimination between the "enlightened" ruling elite and those who refuse to conform to the new global agenda? Contemporary developments suggest that such a scenario is well underway. In April 1975 the Merv Griffin Show aired a discussion about a drug offender who had been sentenced by a Detroit judge to four years of TM. When Merv asked for his opinion, Maharishi enthusiastically endorsed that judge's decision with this shocking statement:

"This is the judgment of the Dawn of the Age of Enlightenment where the man is forced to develop his pure consciousness by law. This is the law of the Age of Enlightenment. By penalty he is forced to evolve."[13] From a website dedicated to Maharishi's mission came this quotation from "The Enlightened Sentencing Project":

There is a trend in contemporary jurisprudence for courts to take a more therapeutic approach to the law and court practice. The mission statement of **The Enlightened Sentencing Project** is to bring light to the field of rehabilitation by teaching offenders high-quality and holistic self-development, health-promoting and stress-reducing techniques, including and especially the Transcendental Meditation technique. Every human being can be liberated from within and every offender should be given the tools to become fully enlightened, empowering him/her to make maximum contribution to society in the most positive way.[14]

As my co-author, David Haddon wrote in our book, _TM Wants You_, "If this is the judgment of the "Dawn" of the New Age, what will be its judgment at high noon?"[15]

One need only look to Maharishi's commentary on the Bhagavad-Gita to find the answer to the preceding question. He describes the warrior Arjuna's counsel to deal with his enemies by attaining _"a state of consciousness_

*which will justify any action of his and will allow him even
to kill in love, in support of the purposes of evolution.*"[16]

Maharishi is communicating a frightening theory to
those who embrace the unitive belief that "All is One." The
act of killing must be only illusory since death cannot kill
the basic underlying consciousness permeating everything,
including man. In this context, killing would only be a ripple
in the ocean of being into which that one life was now being
dunked. Or perhaps it would be a kind of macabre
midwifery, helping a soul on to his next incarnation.

It is important to digest these statements carefully
because they hit at the core of much of the New Mentality,
for its agenda undoubtedly appeals to those who enjoy the
exercise of political power. Such a "ruling elite" could bring
about its program through a well-planned national
emergency. A statement posed during a convocation of
globalists in San Francisco, Sept. 14, 1994, leaves little room
for guesswork: *"We're on the verge of global transformation.
All we need is the right major crisis and the nation will
accept the New World Order."*[17]

A "right crisis" could very well be world hunger. One
day while sitting in the sauna, the Lord spoke to me these
almost audible words: "Most of the world is hungry. Whoever
solves the hunger problems of the world will control the
world." Such transformation could be implemented through
martial law and a "restructuring" of society with economic
sanctions. As for the ethos behind such slavery, Maharishi
envisioned this unifying principle: *"The ignorant will be
made enlightened by a few orderly, enlightened people
moving around. Nature will not allow ignorance to prevail.
It just can't. Non-existence of the unfit has been the law of
nature."*[18] In his interpretation of the Bhagavad-Gita,
Maharishi states that "men" are those who have realized...the

"truth" and "*one who has not realized the truth...does not deserve to be called a man.*"[19] According to Maharishi, "truth" is realized by means of TM, and the "unfit" are those subhumans who refuse to embrace this principle.[20]

WORLD PLAN

A close examination of the World Plan discussed by Maharishi during the Fiuggi teacher training reveals an attempt to change the collective awareness of everyone on the planet. This design proposed to pair one teacher of TM (called a "governor") with one thousand people on earth, to instruct and mentor them in TM. The plan was later revised. One TM initiator gleefully predicted that when the World Plan is finally implemented, "all job applications will feature the question, 'Are you a meditator?'"[21]

When Maharishi made his announcement about the World Plan, many of us left the auditorium in stunned silence and shock. Although extremely troubled by it, no one wanted to rock the boat by openly discussing it and thereby jeopardizing their chances for becoming a TM teacher. But I heard one woman say, "If this world-wide plan is implemented, it had better be right, or we are all in deep trouble." A little red light inside me was flashing. A movement was underway, like a giant invisible undertow pulling humanity en masse beyond safe and familiar shores. Where it would take us, no one was quite sure.

An article written by an SCP staff member summarizes the dangers inherent in the TM movement:

> The mentality of this movement displays every red flag in the textbook of psycho-social pathology: the familiar themes of a-New-Age-is-dawning, follow-our-leader-no-matter-what, we-know-best-for-you, death-is-not-

important, and down-with-the-opposition, which have consistently adorned the abominations of humanity's political history.[22]

Today, Maharishi's World Plan has greatly expanded. The movement now believes that only the square root of one percent of the world's population needs to practice the advanced "TM Sidhi" program to produce what is referred to as the "Maharishi effect." The organization envisions the formation of a kind of invisible psychic government with even more expanded aspirations of capturing the seat of world influence. Based on the Vedic belief that the center point of any building, city, or nation is its most powerful and strategic focus, they have set about to establish Washington Township, Smith County, Kansas as that 480-acre center of the U.S. They call this site "Brahmasthan" (geographical center) of America, home to the US Peace Government and its president and quantum physicist Dr. John Hagelin, Minister of Science and Technology of the "Global Country of World Peace." On March 28, 2006, this new World Capital of Peace was inaugurated as the national center of "coherence and harmony" at Washington Township. They believe that this new capital will make America "invincible." It's an interesting idea, but is it based on reality? If not, its acceptance reveals a deception of enormous magnitude. It boils down to how you define peace and raises the question: peace at what price? The plan is to create peace-generating groups around the world at the local, national, and international levels. It is believed that by sending peace-keeping "experts" into each of these areas a powerful wave of peace will cause warfare and terrorism to cease, silently and effortlessly. Here are their immediate goals:

1) Establish a group of over 500 peace-creating experts in Iowa near Maharishi's University of Management.

2) Host a group of 8,000 peace-creating experts to bring an influence of harmony and unity around the world, with the goal of effectively defusing stress behind all global conflicts. One thousand of those peace experts will reside in Washington Township, Smith County, Kansas.

3) Establish a permanent central group of 40,000 peace-creating experts to be situated on the banks of the Ganges River in India. This group would be larger than any other peace group gathered anywhere in the world by a power of 25 times.

4) Set up 3,000 Peace Palaces in the largest cities of the US, each constructed in accord with special Vedic architectural mandates. Each Peace Palace will house 100 – 200 peace-creating experts. They will offer many varied programs, purportedly to reduce stress, increase health, and unfold the full mental potential of every citizen.

Although the TM-Sidhi program went through a long period of relative quiescence, it seems to be resurfacing because of the threat of terrorism. Any rise in world tensions could fuel a much greater push for their global agenda, with the emphasis on unity, peace at all costs, and personal "moral" responsibility to "save the planet," etc. Today the organization hopes to enlist adherents from every segment of society, especially the educated, influential, and wealthy. They must first gain credibility by convincing the public that such peace-keeping efforts can be scientifically verified.

The problem with the peace research is that the studies are all short term, with no proof of long term benefits. Some of the research has been contested already, such as a recent study on the TM-Sidhi program in the Middle East (please refer to: http://www.behind-the-tm-facade.org/maharishi_effect-mdefect-lebanon.html.

The TM organization does not acknowledge alternate explanations for the phenomena in question. It is important to interpret evidence clearly. As most of us are aware, any number of variables can be manipulated to suit a particular agenda. An excerpt from the Markovsky & Fales study states, *"As it stands, causal linkages from individual TM practitioners to, for instance, a diminished likelihood of Nebraskans wrecking their cars, are hidden in a very 'black box.'"* In other words, the possibility of the TM theory being full of holes is very likely. There are many gaps in the causality chain all the way from group meditation to the area presumed affected (http://www.uspeacegov.org/structure.html). In summary, though they admit to the benefits of other approaches like prayer and different forms of meditation, it is still strongly maintained that only the TM-Sidhi program can bring sufficient change.

SPIRITUAL BACKLASH

At the seminar on "Slowing Down the Aging Process," I explained to two Catholic Dominican sisters about the deception of TM and the Antichrist, the coming new world religion, and the one world government. No doubt the Lord put me there next to them to warn them. In the lobby afterwards, I visited with Evangelos, leader of the Christananda community and told him I thought this humanistic program was deceptive. It was clear that we did not share a common concern when he said, "Well, they have

free choice, don't they? Don't be afraid." I was afraid all right–
for them–and couldn't help grieving for the many who are
seduced by these lies.

Going to the "Aging Process" seminar and
confronting such heavy darkness must have caused no
small spiritual backlash. When I went out to the parking
lot to my car, the antenna was bent over. Furthermore,
after arriving home from the seminar a large, heavy
metallic bed frame propped up against the wall suddenly
fell without a nudge and missed me by a fraction of an
inch, chopping my meditation prayer bench in half.
Evidently it had not felt like falling the whole time I was
away, until I got home! It was a close call.

The next morning while jogging, I was even more
convinced that these mishaps were more than
coincidences. Bio, the neighbor's dog, suddenly ran in
between my feet and sent me flying through the air. When
I landed on the cement, I gashed my hip and injured my
hand. After I managed to stand up, I noticed that the back
window of my car was broken and everything in the car
was ransacked or stolen. When I considered the amazing
series of events immediately following this preview into
the plans of the adversary, I realized that the burgeoning
New Age culture has an incredibly dark side. Sometimes
the spiritual warfare can get dangerous. It is always best to
go with someone and to get prayer covering.

RELIGIOUS RELATIVISM

Today's spiritual climate is filled with many forms of
pagan mystery religions, spiritism, and doctrines of various
mixtures. This situation has occurred throughout the
history of man, but it is becoming increasingly prevalent

today. The seduction of Christianity at its very core is a very serious matter. Paul gave the following warnings to believers,

> *"Beware lest any man cheat you through philosophy and empty deceit, according to the tradition of men, according to the basic principles of the world, and not according to Christ. For in Him dwells all the fullness of the Godhead bodily; and you are complete in Him, who is the head of all principality and power."*
>
> (Colossians 2:8-10)

> *"Let no one cheat you of your reward, taking delight in false humility and worship of angels, intruding into those things which he has not seen, vainly puffed up by his fleshly mind."*
>
> (Colossians 2:18)

Paul was faithful to a simple, pure Gospel—in its truth rests its power.

16

Encounters of the God Kind

MEETING OF THE WAYS

*I*n San Francisco every year there was a gathering called "Meeting of the Ways." Some of us from SCP attended this, and we witnessed to many people there. Like the Davis Whole Earth Festival, this featured a colorful panorama of spiritual organizations from the San Francisco Bay area.

One of the highlights was an on-stage panel of gurus. They were participating in an open-ended discussion of the many paths leading to "enlightenment," with a big emphasis on tolerance and unity among all. I sat in the back and prayed with several Christians from SCP, binding in the name of Jesus all lying spirits and influences. Within minutes of beginning to pray in this manner, the gurus began to dissimulate, feigning oneness and light, but appearing less and less unified as they vied for "favored guru status." The phoniness was deafening. It was an object lesson of the power of prayer to expose hidden things in the light of truth.

As I walked around the many display booths, a man called out to me to try his alpha wave feedback machine. He claimed that this machine could train your mind to produce alpha waves and so develop a mellow, meditative, or calm state of mind. The meter also registered the level of other kinds of brain waves, such as delta and theta. I was excited to get on this machine and to show the powerful effect centering on the Lord Jesus Christ has on the whole person—body, soul, and spirit.

After focusing on Jesus and inwardly worshipping Him for a few moments, I felt His presence. When he attached the machine to me, it showed that I had effortlessly passed beyond alpha waves to strong delta waves, and even to theta, which is a very deep dream-like, or visionary state of mind. He wanted to know what kind of meditation I was doing, and I told him it was just the wonderful, deep peace and spiritual life that Jesus freely gives. He was speechless.

WISDOM, TIMING, AND COMPASSION

Why do I sometimes enjoy going to events that clearly diverge from the solid Biblical teachings I follow? It is because I am refreshed by the intense desire I see in these spiritual seekers for a more complete, integrated existence. They are often quite sincere and passionate in their pursuit of God even though they are yet unable to embrace Jesus fully. I had not witnessed much spiritual passion in many of the Christian churches I had attended. I identified with these spiritual seekers because they reminded me of the days when I was lost and without Christ, but hungering for truth.

The Lord can use us any time to witness about His love and to exemplify that love to others. Once I was walking along Telegraph Avenue in Berkeley. I overheard a Jewish man named Martin telling an acquaintance how his apartment had been broken into by a junkie who started choking him and demanding his money. Martin had no money, but someone had spread a false rumor that he had a lot of money and the junkie didn't believe him. He started to crush Martin's larynx. The intruder then took his cat and brutally killed it before his eyes. As Martin described what happened, he started weeping. He had raised the cat from a tiny kitty, and it was even more faithful than a dog. It would follow him around the house and carry things to him, and now it was dead.

Before meeting Martin, I had been talking with a brother from our church, who offered me some bread. I took four slices and asked Martin if he would like a sandwich and he said, "Sure." So we walked down Telegraph Avenue to "Ma's Revolution" where I bought some cashew butter and spread it on the bread slices as we sat down and talked. He said he was about 50 years old and that he used to tutor physics Ph.D. candidates when he was 14 years old. Obviously he had been a child prodigy. Later he worked with a famous man (not Edward Teller) in developing the A-bomb. He said he felt a personal share of guilt for the thousands of deaths resulting from the bombing of Hiroshima and Nagasaki.

I asked him if he realized that Jesus Christ of Nazareth loved him and created him for a special purpose? At first he seemed quite skeptical but as we talked, he became more interested and started listening. He was touched by concepts like "holiness" and "righteousness" in a world where everyone, as he put it, is out for an "eye for an eye, a tooth for a tooth." When I told him that Jesus forgave him and would wash his guilt away if he would simply pray for forgiveness, he looked shocked. He asked, "This is so simple. Why hasn't anyone ever told me this before?" There on the sidewalk, I introduced him to Jesus as we prayed, and I could really sense that he experienced God. Afterwards, he began to come to our church.

One day I brought Martin a large print Bible because he wore thick glasses and had a hard time reading. He lived alone except for his pet python, which he kept in a strong glass cage—he loved snakes. Martin also wrote poetry and was a good friend of Julia Vinograd, a well known Berkeley street poet. A couple of weeks later I went back to his apartment to check up on him because we had not seen him in church. A neighbor friend of his told me that he had died the day before. This was only one month after I had shared with him about the gift of eternal life.

You never know how timely a witness may be. Whether we realize it at the time or not, the issue is always eternal life or eternal death. Jesus said that He saw the multitudes, and His heart was moved with compassion. They appeared faint and weary and were as sheep without a shepherd. How moved with compassion for people are we? We cannot let the pressures of daily life crowd out many golden opportunities that slip away into eternity, never to be retrieved! Everyone needs to ask God for "divine appointments."

One day I was walking near the Berkeley campus and had a half-eaten sandwich and carton of egg salad in my hand. The thought occurred to me that someone nearby might be hungry. I wondered who it could be. When I continued down the street, my good friend Chris appeared to be the one, so I went up to him and extended the food to him. He said, "Praise God! I was just praying to the Lord for food because I haven't eaten all day." But the story doesn't end here.

As Chris finished off the sandwich, we saw a guy take off all his clothes. He stood there for about five minutes stark naked. Berkeley is famous for "naked" stories. A few of us started praying that the Lord would intervene. About a minute later, he strolled through a crowd of about 50 people and stood before us, saying "Hi." Chris looked right at him with the power of conviction. "Put on your clothes," he said. "I don't have to tell you why; you know why." The naked man's face became a contortion of conflicting forces. As he turned around and left, the dark side had won a temporary victory until the police came and made him dress.

This guy had seen Chris at the free meal served near the campus and had recognized something different in him. Later he told Chris that a voice had been telling him to take off his clothes. Chris told him that the voice was the devil's. The two of them walked up to the Berkeley hills to a nice resting spot where they were able to read some literature about Jesus. When they got to the part about the crucifixion, God touched his heart and he broke down crying and accepted Jesus into his life. He was Jewish, but, in that moment, became a "Messianic Jew."

A few nights later Chris and a few others and I were walking along and a man just bumped into us. We sensed God's purpose, told him about Jesus, and invited him to ask Christ into his heart. He said that the devil was really in control of his life and that he needed the Lord, so he got down on his knees right there on the sidewalk and was saved. When he stood up he looked 100% better. He started coming to our fellowship meetings.

The Jesus Movement of the 70s was a wonderful time to learn about Christ. The glory of God's presence and life-changing power spilled over from the pulpit and the pews into the streets and into peoples' homes. There were planned as well as impromptu spiritual happenings everywhere, resulting in many salvations and rededications of lives. The hippies-turned-Christians had an advantage in that they had not yet succumbed to a "hardening of the categories" that afflicted some of the established church.

Indeed, their drugs and meditations had obliterated *all* boundaries. They had had their fill of deceptive worldly wines, but still they thirsted. Once they discovered the satisfying and exquisite **living water** of the King, they were willing to go anywhere to get it. I believe that the outpouring of God's grace that we saw in the 70s was just a foretaste of the revival that will affect the entire world.

SUPERNATURAL PROTECTION

Berkeley can be a rough place, and several times the Lord supernaturally protected me from certain assault on the streets. One time when I was walking down the street carrying a long-strapped leather purse, a stern inward voice clearly prompted me, "Quickly, put your purse strap around your neck." As I did this, I saw a man standing nearby with his hands positioned to grab my purse. He became immobilized as I looked at him with a sense of God's authority. Miraculously, I passed by untouched.

Another time I was walking down a dark street alone near a public park area, admittedly not a wise thing to do. A young man approached me from the opposite direction. As he passed by, he reached around and grabbed my behind. I sensed I needed to see whether he was following me, and he was. Slowly and seemingly nonchalantly, I crossed the street to the nearest apartment building where I knocked on the door. I told the people I was being followed, and they called the police.

A third and potentially very scary situation presented itself one day when I had answered an ad in the newspaper for a second-hand piano. The piano didn't particularly interest me, but as I turned around to leave, I noticed that five or six men had gathered in the living room to watch a porn movie. Immediately, God's wonderful protective Spirit came over me like a blanket, and I knew I would get out unharmed. Acting as though absolutely nothing was wrong, I told them that I would let them know later if I wanted the piano and quickly left. These and other experiences, too numerous to mention, reveal that God is in charge of our lives, and He has committed Himself to protecting and caring for us. That is good news and one of the great benefits of belonging to Him.

I feel that God wants our hearts to understand that He will direct us and protect us from many from dangers, especially in these end times. He allowed me to go through these things so that I could encourage others to trust Him for divine assistance when facing obstacles that seem insurmountable.

A CLOSER LOOK

In the midst of all of these adventures and opportunities, God was behind the scenes as a divine matchmaker, but He didn't seem to be in a great hurry. One day the Lord told me to take a closer look at Joe and to see Jesus in Him. I began to realize that this friend was to be my husband. There was just one problem—I was not _in love_ with him. One day as I was sitting on a bus, I told God about my misgivings. Suddenly, the Lord poured overwhelming love into my heart for Joe, and from then on I was in love with him, but I knew where the love originated. This romantic attachment was like a magnet drawing me closer to Jesus.

In spite of our growing friendship, Joe remained strangely aloof. One day I asked him point blank where I stood with him. He thought about it and the next day told me that we were just friends. Then he said he felt we should

192 *Authentic Enlightenment*

stop seeing each other because he did not want to "disappoint" me. God's many promises about Joe being my husband some day were surely being tested by fire! About half a year or more went by. In church one day, my pastor gave me this word, "God is turning the tide. Even though for a while circumstances will look opposite, it is a trial and testing of your faith. You have passed the test. You have stood firm, and now it is about to come to pass."

In the "Song of Songs" there is the description of a time of separation between the Bride and her Beloved, a very painful time and difficult to endure. I found out, though, that in God I can risk loving first, because God has already demonstrated His love for me. Conversely, we cannot truly give what we have not first received. The Lord taught me so much of His faithfulness and encouragement during this time. I learned many lessons about how we must walk by faith, not by sight. In spite of my involvement in the many activities surrounding my new faith, I had allowed myself to slip into a somewhat bored and worldly state. It was a question of my love for Jesus. This trial of waiting for Joe was designed to bring me out of lukewarmness back to my "first love," so I would put Him above even my most precious human love. Otherwise, my deep affections for Joe easily could have supplanted my love for Christ.

The turning process was gradual: more regular times of prayer and contact with God in the night hours, more sharing Christ during the day. Nothing of eternal value is ever won without a great price. There was a work of God done on me that year, not the sort of preparation I had expected—it seldom ever is—but I think I really grew from it.

In August, 1980 the Lord said, "It is almost ready, Vail." But waiting for Joe was like looking for the Lord's appearing. It never seemed to materialize! One day the Lord said, "Something romantic will happen in December." On the last day of December when I arrived home, there was a bouquet of flowers with a note from Joe inviting me to a New Year's party and church service. The next evening we had a dinner date. Another day there was walking, shopping, movie, and coffee house and the next day, lunch.

One bright day Joe asked my roommate and me if we would meet him for lunch at one of Berkeley's snazzy, health-oriented restaurants. I had my sprout sandwich half way up to my mouth when he announced that he was going back to Arkansas permanently to live and that he would be leaving soon. The sandwich never got eaten. I was totally shocked. That night, however, Jesus gave me a vision of Joe walking in a straight line away from me until I could hardly see him anymore, but then running straight back to me. So I had the assurance to take me through this one! I knew that God would not let me down.

After several months of waiting, God fulfilled his promise to me. Joe began writing and calling me, and finally he invited me to come to visit him in Arkansas. I liked Arkansas very much, and Joe proposed to me after three days. I had only two months to sell my house, plan for the wedding, and move away from California to my new home in Arkansas. For about a year and a half my life was fulfilled being Joe's wife and teaching a couple of piano students. Then came a special blessing: we discovered that at age forty I was to have a baby. David Carruth was born on the eleventh day of the eleventh month at eleven o'clock! Eleven is a number that, according to dream interpretation symbolism, refers to the "prophetic." This was triply prophetic!!!

Our greatest revelations are usually tested. Several months after David was born I had a vision of him with a fatal injury to his head. He appeared to be about nine years old; his eyes were rolled back, and he looked dead. The vivid impression lasted for two days. I walked around in a daze feeling that I had already lived through this tragedy, it was so vivid. As I sought the Lord, it occurred to me that perhaps God sometimes allows us to see a tragedy *so that it can be averted through prayer.* So I prayed that God would intervene and spare David's life. I prayed that whatever happened, God would get the glory, and I lifted up this concern every day for six years!

SEVERELY PRUNED

I loved my life as a wife and new mother and threw myself totally into enjoying and nurturing my baby. However, two months after David was born problems developed. All the changes in our lives, work, and ministry took a toll on my strength. I began to experience chronic insomnia that was so severe that I could get only about two hours of broken sleep at night. I think anti-depressants helped a little but proved to be addictive, and I could not get off of them for a long time. The problem was exacerbated by hidden allergies resulting from past overuse of antibiotics. My diet only complicated matters. I had consumed dairy products by the gallon, thinking that it was good for the baby. Dairy allergy was one of the main contributors to my deplorable condition at the time. I did not realize that many sicknesses have spiritual roots. It would not be fair if I did not give some credit for this discovery to the ministry of Pastor Henry W. Wright and his wonderful team. He is the author of the now famous book, *A More Excellent Way.* Through this book thousands have experienced amazing freedom from oppression and even life threatening illnesses. Even before this book was in print, amazing results were being widely reported based on the things they teach.

During the days of my environmental illness (severe allergies) when I thought that I would surely wind up in the hospital in an antiseptic germ-free bubble, I was given the phone number of a woman in San Francisco who had been healed through this ministry. Over the phone she told me that there is an essential underlying cause of environmental illness, and that it is a spirit of fear. She encouraged me to contact this ministry, but I did not follow through at that time. However, after the phone call I sat down and told God that though I did not understand all about this spirit of fear, I wanted Him to free me from it if that was my problem. First I repented of fear, then I bound this spirit using the powerful name of Jesus. To my utter amazement I witnessed a sooty, black cloud rise up off of me spiritually. There were times when I had to stand firm on my deliverance from this illness, but the problem never returned. However, I still had chronic fatigue. Using the same principle two weeks later, I asked God to heal me of the tiredness, binding any attitudes related to fear, and it left as well.

Several years later I was divinely led to attend one of the many week long seminars offered by the ministry team at Pleasant Valley Church in Thomaston, GA. To my complete surprise the woman I had called years before in San Francisco, Marcia Fisher, was on their staff along with several of her friends from the San Francisco area. All of them had been healed of environmental illness at around the same time. I spent my first week there in deliverance for myself, and the second week I learned how to apply the powerful principles of deliverance for others. At the end of my second week, Marcia invited a group of us out to see the sights and later for ice cream. Now dairy was one of my taboo foods as it would usually make me very sick. I prayed and then dared to order a gigantic Rum Raisin ice cream cone. After enjoying this treat, I did not experience one negative effect. I'm not saying it is healthy to have ice cream all the time, but we were happy to learn that such an occasional indulgence would not cause us to become deathly ill! For this I truly give God thanks. Rum Raisin is still my favorite ice cream.

Since my stay at Pleasant Valley I have enjoyed much greater freedom and quality of life as well as the privilege of helping others. I encourage anyone who has been involved in New Age, witchcraft, or occult involvement to seek deliverance counseling. Although such help is widely available, you probably would find no better place than Pleasant Valley. It might just give that extra help to clean out the hidden cobwebs and curses that have passed onto you because of unwittingly venturing out into spiritually dark areas.

Through all of these various challenges in my life, God was teaching me many lessons of faith. For a long time I felt utterly abandoned by God and alone. No one, not even my husband, really understood my distress. But I knew that Jesus had already experienced everything I was going through and He did not want me to carry my burdens alone. By rigorously applying the Holy Scriptures to my life, I was discovering real help which would eventually guide me out of my trouble. Formerly I relied too much on mystical experience, but now I was beginning to build my spiritual "house" on a more solid foundation. I was learning to rest in the Lord and to lean on Joe who stood faithfully by me even when my problem strained our marriage. And I was slowly learning to integrate all of the new changes in my life, one day at a time.

One Sunday in August 1985 a prophetic word came forth from someone in the congregation: "I am taking the bare bones of your life and clothing them with flesh. You have been greatly laid bare and pruned. But I have stood you on your feet and I have made you whole again. You will not go back, but I am calling you to come forth with strong hands, and I will use you." That promise of *eventual* deliverance continued to strengthen me even when my situation still looked bleak.

DIVINE INTERVENTION

After Joe finished his studies at Regent University, we returned to Ft. Smith, Arkansas, where he became the principal of a small Christian school. Meanwhile, I was praying daily that God would protect David from the head injury I had seen years before. One day I was half dozing in the family car when a supernatural light seemed to fill the car. Out of the light I heard a voice telling me, "When a baby in the womb has reached six months in its development, it can live on its own. David is now six years old. You have prayed and sought me for David's life and I have heard your prayers. You can stop praying now; David will be all right."

After three more years had passed, Joe and I were having an end-of-the-school deck party for the teachers. We were enjoying ourselves, when I heard a crash and a sickening thud. David had taken a misstep off of our carport and fallen about nine feet, hitting the back of his head on a concrete sidewalk. He was delirious and the doctors at the hospital thought that he had received a basal skull fracture. Remembering the Lord's promise to me that "David will be all right," I opened a small Bible I now carry around with me. It fell open to Matthew 10:29-31:

Are not two sparrows sold for a copper coin? And not one of them falls to the ground apart from your Father's will. But the very hairs of your head are all numbered. Fear not, therefore; you are of more value than many sparrows.

Our assistant pastor came in and asked us how David was doing. I chose not to believe the dire prognosis, but instead said I thought that David would be all right. Within five minutes the doctors came down from their examination and said, "We don't understand it, but there is no fracture. Everything seems to be all right." After a night in the hospital, David was back on his feet the next day, running and playing. We have a wonderful and awesome God! What an example of the power of interventional prayer!

After two more years I conceived again at age 42, but I lost the baby at 8 weeks. In the hospital where I had the miscarriage, a young woman who shared the room with me was dying from a brain tumor. She had two small children at home. Extensive surgery had resulted in blindness in one eye and paralysis on one side of her body. She was scheduled for further brain surgery. I told her how Jesus had healed me of a spinal curvature and asked if she would like me to pray for her. When Joe arrived at the hospital, we both prayed for her, and then we enlisted the prayer help of our home fellowship.

When we called her the next day we learned that the Lord had healed her and that exploratory surgery and a CAT scan had found no evidence of any cancer anywhere. She took this as a wake-up call from God and started attending church again. She regained her sight, had no more paralysis, and was able to return to her two small children. None of this would have happened had I not lost my baby. I am reminded of the scripture, *"And we know that all things work*

together for good to those who love God, to those who are
the called according to His purpose" (Romans 8:28).

I have shared these stories of the early days of my
Christian life to encourage your faith in both the kindness
and the discipline of God. He loves us so much and wants
to encourage us even when things look hopeless. Many
troubles face our nation and world. God is trying to lessen
some of the effects of our national reaping and sowing, but
He needs us to pray and intercede as never before. He is
saying to all people that we must redeem the time. The
sand in the hourglass of our lives is slipping away quickly.
We must see the lateness of the hour and make the necessary
changes in order to obey Him in whatever He is telling us
to do and to be. God sometimes has to allow drastic
measures to get our attention.

I found out that I can be totally honest with God and
He will not send a lightning bolt upon me. During one of
my desperate times, I told God how discouraged I felt. He
said, "If you feel weak and discouraged, know that the Lord
disciplines those He loves. Keep on seeking Me and do not
quit. You'll be set completely free, and you will be restored
and healed." He also said something that gave me great
hope: "To the extent that you have stumbled today, I am
there to pick you up." He will come through for you, too,
if you hold fast and do not doubt. My experience confirms
that what He has promised, He will do.

Time and space would be insufficient to tell you in
great detail about all the other challenges I endured and
overcame through faith, thanks to the goodness and mercy
of my heavenly Father. The saga of how God fulfilled His
many promises to me, the unfolding of my life as a late-
blooming wife and mother, and other great things I've seen
God do will have to appear in a sequel to this book. It is

sufficient to say that if I had continued living the New Age/ TM way, I would still be spiritually lost and light years away from the person I am today.

If my life could be summed up in one phrase, it would be "in pursuit of God." Undoubtedly, even during the dark days of my youth, there was an unseen work of God's grace through the prayers of my grandmother and other family members. I am astounded constantly at the faithfulness of God to answer prayers to bring me through the storms of the world and all of its glitz and glitter. He alone can satisfy our hearts and complete us. This is the only God, my Master and Savior, Jesus Christ. He is the one I love with all my heart, and as time goes on, I am more and more assured of His love for me. He has never failed me and has always proven Himself trustworthy.

17

Things I
Never Wanted to Believe

BUT I DO NOW

*W*hen I embarked on my TM journey, I was unaware of the warnings in the Bible not to involve the names of other gods in a spiritual quest. During the teacher-training course, I discovered that each so-called meaningless sound (mantra) was actually the name of one of thousands of Hindu deities. I now know these 'gods' are simply the product of human imagination, or they are demonic beings masquerading as gods—fallen angels who rebelled against the one true God. The Biblical revelation is clear about the deity of Jesus Christ and His preeminent position as Savior: *"Nor is there salvation in any other, for there is no other name under heaven given among men by which we must be saved"* (Acts 4:12). This is not a welcomed teaching in today's world, but Jesus did not seek to win any popularity contests. He differentiated His "way" of salvation from all other paths:

> *"All who ever came before Me are thieves and robbers, but the sheep did not hear them. I am the door. If anyone enters by Me, he will be saved, and will go in and out and find pasture. The thief does not come except to steal, and to kill, and to destroy. I have come that they may have life, and that they may have it more abundantly."* (John 10:8-10)

202 Authentic Enlightenment

According to the teachings of the Bible, we are not to believe every experience, but to test the spirit behind it to see if it is from God. Every spirit that confesses that Jesus, the Messiah, has come to earth in the flesh is authentic. But every spirit that denies this is of the spirit of Antichrist. My experience of the tree spirits was just one of many serious deceptions, as I was to discover later.

For instance, Jesus warned about the use of meaningless repetition when we meditate or pray: *"And when you are praying, do not use meaningless repetition, as the Gentiles do, for they suppose that they will be heard for their many words...Do not be like them, for your Father knows what you need before you ask Him"* (Matthew 6:7-8, NAS). In the verses immediately following this warning, Jesus demonstrated the value and effectiveness of the Lord's Prayer with which we are all familiar. I discovered that this prayer has power on many different levels, ranging all the way from rational one-on-one communication, to experiencing deeper rest affecting the spiritual, emotional, and physical levels. (The rest of Christ is much deeper and better than what is promised through TM.) All of this is achieved immediately and progressively without suppressing the faculties of the mind.

One of the things I used to believe was that Jesus and His early disciples must have used a secret meditation technique (this is a very common New Age belief). This viewpoint ostensibly explains away all the miracles He performed. It was common for many of my hippie friends to try to cast Jesus into the role of "super-hippie" or guru, but somehow the description never seemed to fit exactly. Maharishi taught that the source of wars and trouble in the world resulted from the gradual loss of transcendental knowledge down through the years, but that every so often the world would be "blessed" by the appearance of an enlightened being (like himself) who would restore this knowledge to mankind.

At the time, I really believed that secret things carry a certain kind of power. It is hard for the mind of a TM meditator to grasp the idea that words read or spoken plainly from the Bible, especially the Name of Jesus, could be filled with a great life-changing power without needing the secret cloak that TM and other occult practices require. After all, the Heavenly Father has the original spiritual blueprint! For every counterfeit there is the real.

> *For thus says the LORD, Who created the heavens, Who is God, Who formed the earth and made it, Who has established it, Who did not create it in vain, Who formed it to be inhabited: I am the LORD, and there is no other. I have not spoken in secret, in a dark place of the earth; I did not say to the seed of Jacob, 'Seek Me in vain'; I, the LORD, speak righteousness, I declare things that are right.*
>
> (Isaiah 45:18-19)

Like good food, the healing and nourishing power of the Word of God has no side effects, down side, or dangers like the "drugging" of occult techniques. The extraordinary divine force that raised Jesus Christ from the dead is the same power working in and through many believers today. Amazingly, this power is not confined to a small fringe group of enlightened believers, but is openly available to all who wholeheartedly trust in Christ. If you try to tell TM meditators this Good News, they may not believe it. This understanding was also veiled from my eyes during my involvement with TM. However, if you seek Him, He will reveal Himself and His Kingdom to you and begin to perfect you into His image and likeness. He promises that all He has been given by the Father can be yours, *in this life* as well as in the life to come. He came to bring many sons and daughters to Glory.

JESUS ONLY

Some may wonder how to respond to sincere seekers of truth who come from a tradition where many gods are worshipped. Sister Gwen Shaw, Founder and President of End-Time Handmaidens, shares an interesting story in her excellent book *Unconditional Surrender.* She tells about a time when she was in India and God told her that an Indian Sadhu (holy man) in a saffron-colored robe would be coming to her to find the way of truth more perfectly. One afternoon as she was enjoying a cup of tea, she looked up and saw the Sadhu. He had traveled many miles, and indeed he was a sincere spiritual seeker. The Lord Jesus had appeared to him. He loved Jesus, but didn't know whether it was all right for him to be praying to any of the deities he had been taught to worship. He related to her how, at times, while performing his Hindu rituals he had actually seen Satan and the chasms of hell. So Sister Gwen spent the afternoon telling him about the way of salvation. After seeking the Lord in prayer about the Sadhu's question, Sister Gwen received this scripture from Matthew 17:8: *"And when they had lifted up their eyes, they saw no one but Jesus only."* This is taken from the experience of Jesus and his three disciples on the Mount of Transfiguration.

In this episode, Peter desired to build three tabernacles, one for Elijah, one for Moses (both prophets of God), and one for Jesus. It was as if Peter wanted to put all three on the same level, when in fact Jesus was far greater. Suddenly a bright cloud surrounded them. When it lifted they saw only Jesus. Gwen Shaw explained to the Sadhu, *"When we are in the mists, we see many great saints and prophets and teachers and gurus and masters. But when the clouds lift from our understanding, then we see only Jesus."*[23] The Sadhu believed this and received "only Jesus" as his true Master, forsaking all others. I have never found a story that better illustrates the exclusivity of Christ's claims to divinity and why we should follow only Him. When we have found that which is perfect, we don't need to keep looking.

THE QUESTION OF SUFFERING

One of the most alluring baits dangling before me when I was a TM meditator was the promise that TM would eventually bring me to a state of consciousness that would eliminate all suffering. I distinctly disliked the message I had always been taught in church that suffering automatically makes one more spiritual (it seemed like the practice of wearing hair shirts). This kind of asceticism is not what Jesus really taught. On the other hand, he never taught that we don't ever have to suffer. Maharishi's view of the mission of Christ reveals an immense distance from the Christian teaching on suffering:

> I don't think Christ ever suffered or Christ could suffer…it is a painless suffering. Those who count upon the suffering, it is a wrong interpretation of the life of Christ and the message of Christ…The message of Christ has been the message of Bliss….[24]

Let's look at the words of the Master Himself. After His crucifixion, Jesus appeared to His disciples on the road

206 *Authentic Enlightenment*

to Emmaus and chided their unbelief, saying, *"O foolish ones, and slow of heart to believe in all that the prophets have spoken! Ought not the Christ to have suffered these things and to enter into His glory?"* (Luke 24:25-26). And consider the exhortation by the apostle Paul: *"You therefore must endure hardship as a good soldier of Jesus Christ"* (2 Timothy 2:3). *"And also if anyone competes in athletics, he is not crowned unless he competes according to the rules"* (2 Timothy 2:5). Again: *"For I consider that the sufferings of this present time are not worthy to be compared with the glory which shall be revealed in us"* (Romans 8:18). But in suffering, a Christian has solid hope. *"...as you are partakers of the sufferings, so also you will partake of the consolation"* (2 Corinthians 1:7). Moreover, *"If we suffer, we shall also reign with Him: if we deny Him, He also will deny us"* (2 Timothy 2:12 KJV).

Although the invitation to come to Christ is accessible to all—easy some might say—the message of a cheap and easy salvation is deceptive. Believing that spiritual growth can be attained without any cost to ourselves can lead to disillusionment, keeping us from a genuine relationship with our Creator. The eternal ramifications of millions swallowing this lie are horrendous.

As we progress in the Christian life, we come to recognize that there is no easy escape from suffering. Being willing to suffer marks the true disciple of Christ. Many desire to follow a bloodless, cross-less gospel (*"another Jesus"*), but the true disciple is willing to follow Jesus no matter what the cost, even if things get rough. There is no greater test of loyalty. Jesus promised that the Comforter (the Holy Spirit) would be with us to help us. *"But he who endures to the end will be saved"* (Matthew 10:22). Those who think that their state of consciousness will save them may need to reconsider.

He is able to shake all things, that only what is founded in Him will stand.

Hardship builds spiritual muscle. What is your hardship today? Many of you are suffering or have attempted to eliminate it through the technique of TM, by changing the nervous system and suppressing the symptoms that signify a deeper problem that TM doesn't even address. But sufferings and trials will always be with us. Many times the Lord will intervene, change, or lift our sufferings and circumstances. Or He will fill our inner being with such joy and strength, we won't focus on our weakness or suffering, but on Him.

If viewed correctly, suffering—though universally detested and feared—can be one of the greatest opportunities for spiritual growth. In the Biblical account of the harsh treatment of Joseph by his brothers, Joseph later said to them, *"But as for you, you meant evil against me; but God meant it for good, in order to bring it about as it is this day, to save many people alive"* (Genesis 50:20). A diamond is formed under great pressure. Silver has to go through the refining fire several times in a furnace. We cannot get away from this truth. If we will patiently and humbly yield to the Lord in these matters, He will exalt us in due time, having found us to be proven and worthy vessels.

When the adversary digs a pit of hurt and disappointment in your life, Jesus stands ready to fill it with a more excellent weight of glory, if you will yield the matter to Him. Nature abhors a vacuum. Either the spiritual excavation will be filled with heaven's wisdom and life, or it will become a pit of bitterness and despair. We talk about giving to God in terms of charity or finances, but the most difficult yet rewarding kind of giving is when we offer to God these deep hurts of the heart. If you make this offering to God with thanksgiving instead of running from them, His heart will be captured by your worship and trust. He will fill that empty place with the new wine of His Presence, heal your wounds, and give your life a renewed sense of purpose. Sufferings can even open up unexpected areas of blessing or opportunity. In any case, you will grow by leaps and bounds; this is an absolute guarantee.

The apostle Paul did not fear suffering: *"The Holy Spirit solemnly testifies to me in every city, saying that bonds and afflictions await me"* (Acts 20:23, NASB). In fact, Paul had a "thorn in the flesh" from which he prayed to be delivered. Although the Lord Jesus often answers our prayers for divine healing, He denied this request in favor of a higher good in Paul's life, so that He could teach Paul things he couldn't learn any other way. If there had been an easier way, God surely would have granted it.

The Psalmist also addressed suffering in a positive light: *"Before I was afflicted I went astray, but now I keep your word...It is good for me that I have been afflicted, that I may learn Your statutes"* (Psalm 119:67, 71). Paul wrote, *"...for I have learned in whatever state I am, to be content:... Everywhere and in all things I have learned both to be full and to be hungry, both to abound and to suffer need"* (Philippians 4:11-12).

Having said all this, we must regard those who suffer with the utmost compassion and to *"weep with those who weep"* (Romans 12:15). We live in a fallen world, and people go through horrendous suffering. Though much of this comes through demonic influence, God's redemptive purpose covers all things. So it never takes Him by surprise when storms and trials hit us. However, we will not always understand why some are rescued in this life and some are not. If we could figure out this mystery, we would be God. Miracles do happen; God does answer prayers, but not always according to *our* expectations.

DEMONS AREN'T NICE

Some of the sufferings we encounter in this life are directly due to the dark forces all around us. It wasn't until after I became a born-again Christian that I realized the goal of these spirit beings. Their purpose is to bring about the ultimate possession and spiritual death of human souls. One thing that will help protect a person is to avoid going to places heavily infested by evil spirits. If you decide to visit an occult group or place of false worship (often unwise, unless you are bearing the truth to them), always go with another person and get prayer covering. Be sure you are in the Lord's will; otherwise presumption can put you in harm's way. There are extremely powerful and malevolent spirits who hate the blood of Jesus, and they will try to put curses on you if you are trespassing on what they consider "their" territory. Again, let me emphasize: demons don't like Christ, and they don't like you…especially if you belong to Christ.

DEMONS DON'T PLAY FAIR

People who are more impressed by spiritual experiences than the balanced guidelines of the Scriptures can be easily deceived. I was such a person at one time. Please be very careful! It is not erroneous or narrow minded to say that spiritual leaders whose teachings do not lift up the deity of Jesus Christ in accordance with the Biblical revelation are in danger of ultimately deifying themselves. Never wanting to view God as a cosmic "cop," I finally realized that there are spiritual laws in the universe put in place by God for our protection and good. Departing from the path just invites trouble. The ultimate price for self-deification is eternal separation from God, a much-too-hefty price to pay for going our own, stubborn way. While some deceivers may not be dressed in white or sit in caves meditating, the evil entities that control them are just as eager to bring you under their influence in exchange for your adulation and praise. Enormous pride can be camouflaged under a humble or ascetic exterior.

SIMPLICITY OF CHRIST

Although human beings love to forge their own way in things, I discovered the hard way that people cannot come to God on their own terms. You cannot enter the portals of heaven by walking through a graveyard. What most people do not realize is that the devil can mimic Christ and appear as *"another Jesus"* or an *"angel of light"* (2 Corinthians 11:4, 14). The Apostle Paul warned us not to stray from the simplicity of the Gospel of Christ.

Many of the followers of the Christian offshoots I looked into were once sincere believers like myself who did not heed God's warnings. They wound up off track. What got me back on the right path was the exercise of repentance, prayer, and the daily study of God's Word. This was my spiritual road map and it proved essential. These are life and death issues. Not only do we need to know what the Bible says, we need to allow the Spirit of God to give us fresh understanding each day for guidance. He will actually "highlight" specific passages in the Bible for us as we read. This is called a *rhema* word. The written word of God in its entirety is called the _Logos_, which is given for general understanding.

SELF-PERFECTIONISM
AND THE CROSS

At one time I believed that New Age deception is only found in TM, Buddhism, astrology, the occult and philosophies of that nature. Although most people can distinguish New Age philosophy from Christian doctrine fairly easily, it is not as simple to recognize deception when it comes into the church itself. Self-perfectionism—striving for perfection through the attainment of spiritual powers apart from the cross of Christ—has always been the goal of the New Age Movement. Christians can also be deceived when they think that manifestations of the gifts of the Spirit indicate a close, holy walk with the Lord. Christians also err through asceticism, legalism, and self-righteous works. The goal of self-perfectionism is the same whether it involves self-effort or the passivity of meditation. Our perfection can come only through Jesus, who referred to Himself as the "narrow gate" (narrow minded to some). The law of gravity is also narrow, but it is best to observe that law.

Thinking that we can attain our own perfection in this life without the work of the cross of Christ reflects both the deep flaw in our human nature and our proud refusal to admit it. I am fully convinced that while most Christians are willing to come to the "salvation cross," many are not willing to take up their "daily cross." This daily cross isn't just a nice idea; it is a necessity. Every day of our lives, through our willingness to defer to the will of God, we are in training for the times of much greater testing. We are not suddenly going to be ready without this consistent preparation. We can only understand this daily cross in the context of a close personal relationship with Christ.

Of course, one does not change overnight. Depending on our background before being saved, certain areas in our lives still need to be "taken for Christ." In the Old Testament, the Bible describes what would happen if land was cleared too quickly of predators. It would allow empty land to exist that could then be taken by something worse. In a similar fashion, God does not overhaul us instantly, but usually step by step, until we can assimilate and adjust to the changes. But that daily cross of obedience marks the true disciple and is what God desires and, indeed, requires of our lives. I believe that a cheap Gospel is one that allows you to "do your own thing" with no sacrifice required. Obedience to Christ is the toughest! It reaches right down to all our hidden motives. But the results and rewards of this path are well worth it. A Christianity without the cross is actually a false religion.

SOMETHING I HAVE ALWAYS BELIEVED

Integrity has been referred to as "the unity of belief and action." Many Christians use theological terms (such as salvation) in what is primarily an abstract, or general, sense. But what relevance can an abstraction have to our lives? As my son, David Carruth, put it:

> In the matter of salvation, incarnating these lofty phrases into our actual 'flesh and blood' existence makes them truly significant to us. This method trans-forms the church-word 'salvation,' with its memorized meaning, into a realized concept evident in each of our lives. Although salvation is an eternal gift, we must "renew and refresh" it to our souls every day.

I hope *Authentic Enlightenment* has adequately described just HOW pragmatic salvation can be; indeed, how God can work through us, inspiring grace, evoking mercy, eliciting the compassion that makes this world a better place to live.

Along this path toward spiritual fulfillment and enlightenment, there are some sign-posts placed by our Creator to enable us to reach our destination without fatalities. For the Christian the practice of TM is forbidden by Scripture, for the Biblical revelation is that of a God who will not condone the worship of other gods. We should not take their names into our lips (Psalm 16:4). He has placed this restriction before us for our protection and good. Here is what God says in His Word, along with a fitting response:

> *I am the Lord your God, who brought you out of the land of Egypt, out of the house of slavery. You shall have no other gods before Me. You shall not make for yourself an idol, or any likeness of what is in heaven above or on the earth beneath or in the water under the earth. You shall not worship them or serve them; for I, the Lord your God am a jealous God, visiting the iniquity of the fathers on the children, and on the third and the fourth generations of those who hate Me, but showing loving kindness to thousands, to those who love Me and keep My commandments.*
> (Deuteronomy 5:6-10, NASB)

> *Oh, how I love Your law! It is my meditation all the day. You, through Your commandments, make me wiser than my enemies; for they are ever with me. I have more understanding than all my teachers, for Your testimonies are my meditation. I understand more than the ancients, because I keep Your precepts.*

I have restrained my feet from every evil way, that I may keep Your word. I have not departed from Your judgments, for You Yourself have taught me. How sweet are Your words to my taste, sweeter than honey to my mouth! Through Your precepts I get understanding; therefore I hate every false way.

(Psalm 119:97-104)

18

Refuge in the Storm

SEEKING GOD'S FACE

*M*any people all over the world have sought God for a revival of true spirituality in the Church and the world. The promised visitation of power spoken of in Joel 2:28 is showing up in many places. Revival brings rejoicing, but let us not forget that this blessing comes with a very costly price—the blood of Jesus Christ and our life of surrender to Him.

> *And it shall come to pass afterward, that I will pour out My spirit upon all flesh; and your sons and your daughters shall prophesy, your old men shall dream dreams, your young men shall see visions....And it shall come to pass, that whoever calls on the Name of the LORD shall be saved.*

> (Joel 2:28, 32)

I am still amazed at how God intervened in my life to satisfy my deep longing for spiritual fulfillment. He wants hearts that are hungry for Him! It has taken a major refocusing effort, aided by God's gracious love and outpouring, to release my own life in order to gain more of His plan, purpose, and calling. I found out that my friend and former roommate, Jan, became stricken with terminal cancer. She called me one day and said that because of the grace and goodness of God, she was experiencing a great outpouring of joy even in the midst of her situation. She prayed over the phone for the Lord's renewing work in my life. The day after talking to Jan on the phone, I was seated alone at the dining room table worshipping the Lord, when suddenly I spontaneously began to laugh for no apparent "reason." Just that morning I had read a scriptural passage about laughing that seemed highlighted for me. That night I slept what seemed like a perfect night's sleep in complete peace. I don't think I woke up once—I believe that significant healing occurred during that laughing episode, sent to me from God. What I think the Lord did was remove my fear of not sleeping. Now if I have insomnia, I just rest and pray. Sometimes I go back to sleep, sometimes I don't. No big deal. Although this experience was very unusual, I have learned not to put God in a box in order to match my preconceptions as long as I follow Biblical guidelines and the "fruit" of it is a growth of God's love in my life.

I would like to share briefly what a young woman, a former devotee of a guru in New York, has to say about false versus true spiritual experiences. First she gives a little of her background. She writes:

> I have had much similar experiences as you, even though I was not in TM, but for the last four years in *Kundalini Shaktipat Yoga.* However, since last summer the Lord has been "rescuing" me, and I have come to realize that it actually is a practice that "numbs" one up, and yes, as I have been closely in contact with these gurus, I have noticed that they sometimes "change," and one can sense a definite something oppressing and strange around them. This is actually fascinating, as many of them have a very good intention, but I do suspect that very strange psychic forces are at work here. What Jesus gives is light, and

encourages true emotion, it is TRUE love, and not these heavy, changing, oppressing, numbing energies. Could the so-called "enlightenment" be partial possession? However, they seem to also "do good things" to their followers, and many Indians (Hindus) are very kind and polite people. This "guru" thing really is some type of a "mind warp." It is like sinking into some type of a state of mind where really strange waves of reality-mind-magic illusion...hit you and it is really hard to keep the mind and thinking clear even after stopping the practices. So I am driving long hours to go to churches where the presence of the Lord is strong enough to help me.

She goes on to describe what she discerns is the difference between occult energies and the spiritual experiences in Christ that she now is having:

Some people malign [some spiritual manifestations] pointing out the similarities to _Kundalini Yoga,_ but personally I think that it is _NOT the same thing._ At church when an anointed preacher lays hands on me I do feel supercharged or filled with love, and yes, my spiritual body responds to it also, but it is somehow "pure" anointing descending softly and cleansing you, not really the "bottom of the spine" creepy thing (grin). Also the kundalini shakti feels heavier and tends to make you numb, even though it also can induce some feeling of well being, even laughter, but the laughter that the Holy Spirit gives comes from the "deep heart", I think. There is true joy and radiance, not a strange "mixture"...I feel that the world does desperately need true anointing to act as an antidote to all sorts of other occult things.

We are exhorted, "Do not despise prophesying." We should not despise the more unusual manifestations of the Holy Spirit, either. Some people do not feel comfortable with it because of the many false experiences and prophecies that

218 Authentic Enlightenment

abound. We must examine everything carefully because sometimes things will be uncertain and we will ask ourselves, is this of God or is it a counterfeit, flesh or spirit? What is needed is discernment, not the polar opposites of gullibility or criticism. The Word of God tells us to hold fast to what is good and to abstain from what is evil. Here is a very good guideline on how to know if something is genuinely from God:

1) You will feel an inner assurance from the Holy Spirit that it is genuine.
2) It will not contradict Scripture.
3) It will uphold the deity, exclusiveness and Lordship of Christ.

If a manifestation meets all three requirements, most likely, you can relax and enjoy what God is giving you without being unduly suspicious or alarmed. God has a lot of gifts and blessings in His basket to hand out to us if we will be like innocent, happy children to receive them!

THE FUTURE

Our preparation for eternity is a close, intimate walk with our Lord and Savior aided by the "antidote" of the true **Presence** and power of God. I found out that is something the cults and the New Age cannot give you. Before Jan went to be with Jesus, she said that she had experienced the greatest year of her life because of this anointing. In the midst of her crisis, she was comforted and did not fear dying. Jan's husband, David, learned, as we all must, "that joy is not the absence of sorrow or pain but the transforming presence of God in the midst of it all." Here is a letter written by a friend of the family the morning after Jan's departure:

A vision concerning Jan began to unfold...a heavenly figure clothed in a long, flowing white robe appeared at the right-hand corner of her bed...inviting her to come home with Him. Then, with an everlasting look of love and tenderness in His eyes, rising from deep within His heart, He reached His hand toward her. Captivated and consumed in His love, she extended her hands toward His. He gently took her hands in His hand and led her home...I do not know why the Lord chose me for this vision, but it is one I shall never forget. It was one of absolute beauty (August 18, 1997).

No one knows the exact future, but we do know who holds the future. The Scriptures tell us that God will reveal to each one of us our own unique set of instructions if we will humble ourselves before Him. True humility is a willingness to make necessary changes in attitude or lifestyle – whatever God desires. In addition to this, God is calling each of His children to be worshippers. He wants us to enter into the secret place of His presence. Jesus did not write a survival manual; He spoke about an imparted Life that cannot die. That is our only true safety in the storms ahead.

SPIRITUAL INTIMACY

I feel strongly that Jesus wants to teach us all more about the power of His love. If you know Christ, your passion for Him should just keep getting deeper the longer you pursue Him. In your times of prayer and meditation, learn to linger and soak in His presence. Don't be in such a hurry. Lovers savor each other's presence with no other agenda than just to be together. Established in authentic, divine love—holy, selfless and full of power—we and the spiritual offspring born of His love will transform a world on the brink of destruction and usher in the Lord of Glory.

I have discovered the joys and benefits of daily "soaking," or "marinating" in the presence of the Lord. It is His greatest pleasure to draw us closer to His heart so that we may cherish a deeper intimacy with Him. It's His love, not theology that changes us for the better. We aren't going to impact our community or world until we can reflect the nature of the One with whom we spend our most important moments. This kind of sweet communion of our soul with Jesus is so wonderful that every day I still run to Him as a bride would anticipate her lover. Hungry for more of the piercing sweetness of His love, I find in Him a satisfaction, peace, and healing better than anything the world has to offer. The Song of Songs recorded in the Bible is not only a moving love epic, it is also a picture of the love of the Bride for her heavenly Bridegroom.

The Scriptures describe a river of life that never runs dry, a wellspring of heavenly joy that comes to us when we are born again. It flows without ceasing because it never stops pouring from the heart of the Father God. Having this river of life within gives us many benefits. We happily come to discover that it empowers, refreshes, strengthens, and calms us. It is a treasure of amazing joy. (Those of you in the New Spirituality, I believe that this is the thing for which many of you have been searching.)

The Bible depicts a conversation between Jesus and a woman at a well. To this woman He said, *"Whoever drinks of this water will thirst again, but whoever drinks of the water that I shall give him will never thirst. But the water that I shall give him will become in him a fountain of living water springing up into everlasting life"* (John 4:13-14).

The Biblical portrayal of Mary and Martha presents a description of two kinds of spiritual seekers, those who pursue active service and those who enjoy quiet contemplation.

Martha was busy with many things, but Mary loved to sit at Jesus' feet, bask in His presence, and hear His words. Jesus did not criticize Martha, for she was doing a good work. However, He commended Mary, because He knew that divine wisdom would be imparted from knowing Him. It is this "better part" that can never be taken away from us. How can we say we love Him and not like to spend time with Him? If time is valuable, a wise investor would lavish it on Him.

Please note that quiet contemplation is not a relaxation technique or a self-help tool. Nor is it a repetitive New Age exercise for emptying the mind. No one is exempt from human error. Contemplating God in a correct, Biblical sense can provide incomparably rich experiences as one grows in intimacy with Him. The influx of Eastern mystical practice indicates a need that the churches have not fully grasped. Many have not yet caught a vision of the very great opportunity before us. We should not be surprised when many spiritually hungry pre-Christian believers attempt to find direct spiritual knowledge through an Eastern technique, self-discipline, or guru. It is a tragedy that they feel they must look elsewhere, because Jesus died to release for his followers the true inner awakening. Within the guidelines of the Holy Scriptures, this awakening brings _Authentic Enlightenment_.

True Biblical meditation has been given divine boundaries, but we should never despise them for they keep us within God's loving parameters and make us accountable to a Source of wisdom much greater than our own. We cannot possibly know ourselves objectively outside of His revelation of truth. Interestingly, the Holy Spirit is referred to as the "Spirit of truth" (John 14:17). He is also called "The Helper" (John 15:26). He came to assist us in our spiritual journey.

I believe that even the old hippies would really appreciate what Jesus has to offer, because His way is truly radical. Following Him in obedience will revolutionize your life. But time is running out! Please hear this wake-up call. We need to quit trying to patch together that ragged, worn-out empty vacuum of a life and lift our eyes to the Creator Himself. He is beyond this created world, including all its "realms." And yet, once we have received Him and are spiritually reborn, the Kingdom of God lies WITHIN us. But our participation in this Kingdom is based on our submission to the King.

Jesus told us that He was going to prepare a place for us, that where He is, we could be also. Now that's an offer too good to refuse. We need to do things His way or we could miss it entirely. It is a matter of divine protocol; after all, He is King! Great treasures and riches are at your disposal, probably sitting on a forgotten shelf somewhere in your house or apartment gathering dust. Why not shake off the dust and open the pages of your Bible to 2 Peter 1:3-4:

> *His divine power has given us everything we need* (do we need TM or yoga?) *for life and godliness through our knowledge of Him who called us by His own glory and goodness. Through these He has given us His very great and precious promises, so that through them you may participate in the divine nature and escape the corruption in the world caused by evil desires.*
>
> (NIV, comment added)

Trying to achieve His glory without revelation of truth is similar to building a bridge with straw. It is often said that a good building must have integrity. It is the same with a person's spiritual being, or "house." Tapping into serpent power at the base of your spine or opening the occult inner eye is futile because the basic flaw in our human nature needs to be addressed. If you want to live eternally, you will have to have integrity (spiritual knowledge PLUS God's transformation power). This is the saving of the soul that can only come by grace from the One who alone is holy and perfect. Without Christ you will miss it!

God is seeking a people who desire to know Him above all else. It is not visions or any kind of supernatural manifestations that will win an intimate place near His heart. Neither will we find the answer from the panoply of this world's offerings, though we search high and low. We need to meditate, think, and act upon the God-breathed wisdom of the Scriptures, for they are an anchor to our soul in times of intense conflict, pain, or pressure. When the chips are down, we can't bank on yesterday's experiences, but on what is truthful and real. The Bible contains many rich and great promises for wholeness, healing, and deliverance.

Psalm 37:4 says, *"Delight yourself in the LORD, and He shall give you the desires of your heart."* Jesus will not withhold any spiritual gift, and the Scripture tells us to earnestly desire the best gifts. But Jesus is saying that without knowing Him personally, such attainment would entrap you, the seeker. He promised, *"Ask, and it will be given to you; seek, and you will find; knock, and it will be opened to you. For everyone* (that means YOU*) who asks receives, and he who seeks finds, and to him who knocks it will be opened"* (Matthew 7:7-8, added emphasis). Does just asking seem too simple? I think you will be astounded at the way He faithfully answers.

If you are tired and thirsty and longing for freedom, if you deeply desire to find a sense of peace and completion, God offers fulfillment. Where the Spirit (*manifest Presence*) of the Lord is, there is liberty. Obviously, in order to advance, you cannot stay where you are (remain in worldly bondage). Going higher may mean that you might have to leave behind some things on which you have relied in order to move forward. Jesus will make it possible. It is His enablement, not your own ability, that overcomes what seems insurmountable. After all, Jesus rose from the dead! When He conquered the grave, He was demonstrating to us that with God, nothing will be impossible. But it takes faith. God Himself has to initiate that faith; we cannot acquire it apart from Him. We need to make an informed choice to believe that God loves us enough to want to help us, rather than turning to an empty spiritual counterfeit for answers. The war of the ages is over the affections of our hearts. The battlefield is the mind. Will you believe? Will you trust Him? The decision is yours. He's given us the freedom to choose. If you are struggling with the faith to believe, ask Him to help you with that. My prayer is this:

Reign in us, God! Forgive us for turning to false solutions that can never bring ultimate answers. Holy Spirit, come and impart Your faith and power that can move mountains, and make us Your agents of change. Lord Jesus, as we take time to bask in Your presence, reveal to us the depth of Your healing love and forgiveness. Let us come to know You more intimately.
— Amen.

May the reader of this book seek to know Christ and discover the transforming power of His love. There is a radical group of people who love God and are filled with His glory. It is my prayer that you will be one of them. Those who know their God will embody and reveal the Source of *Authentic Enlightenment* to a spiritually hungry world.

Appendix

FINAL INSTRUCTIONS

Stanley (the individual I mentioned earlier in this book) outlined some important principles in a testimonial tract, which are worth quoting at length:

> There are some important things that one must know which are the essence of timeless truth revealed by God: First, that Jesus Christ of Nazareth is the only way to God. Secondly, the ancient Hebrew and Greek scriptures of the Bible have been directly inspired by God, and they are the only foundational scriptures to be trusted. By careful study, you will see that the Scriptures deny the doctrines of reincarnation, astrology, and all psychic and spiritual experiences accessible to man that do not center on the person of Jesus Christ, the Father, and the Holy Spirit. It is very important to understand that you do not have God within you until you have received Jesus Christ as Lord and Savior. Study this pattern of truth.

> Ask Jesus to enter your heart, forgive your sins by His atonement and set your feet on the path of His call. Read the Bible and enter into fellowship with God's people.

> Renounce all spiritual involvements outside of Christ, walk in the freedom of joy of His presence and you will live. Jesus will not deny you spiritual fulfillment, and in fact He wishes to use you as an instrument of His power, love, and all fruits of the Spirit (Galatians 5:22-25).

Ask Him to baptize you in the fire of the Holy Spirit. Desire the spiritual gifts God has for you, and you will be used to perform miracles and healings of supernatural love. Ask Christ to give you all that He has for you, and you will never be lacking in anything spiritual or natural.

CHECK LIST OF OCCULT ACTIVITIES

If you have been involved in any occult activities in your past, you will need to renounce them to break free from the hold of the psychic forces upon your consciousness. This is so the Spirit of God can fill your life, and so that there will be no unholy mixtures. It is important that you confess these activities to God and ask for His forgiveness and cleansing, even if you did not think you were doing anything wrong. Repentance and forgiveness are two of the most powerful spiritual tools there are. You will need freedom and deliverance from demonic influence associated with TM, the New Age movement, or anything occult.

Although you are not guilty of the sins of your ancestors, their involvement can influence your family line and cause many problems. So if you know for certain that members of your family—past or present—have practiced any of these things, you may repent of this also, asking the Lord to cleanse you of all defiling influences and demonic control. Having done this, you can then experience *"the liberty by which Christ has made us free"* (Galatians 5:1). To deal with any remaining problem areas, there are many excellent Christian counselors specializing in deliverance who would be happy to pray with you. It is my personal experience that good deliverance counseling is very effective and necessary to get free from the influence of any former occult activity.

Here is a check list you may find very useful. Do not be amazed if you see on this list some things you thought were perfectly harmless. Just because they are popular in today's culture does not make them right.

Have you or any family member or ancestor...

1. been involved with fortune telling, tarot cards, astrology, or palm reading?
2. been to a hypnotherapist, practiced self-hypnotism, or used pendulums?
3. read tea leaves or crystal balls?
4. practiced yoga?
5. attended a séance or a spiritualist meeting?
6. believed in reincarnation or had a "life reading?"
7. played with a Ouija board even if it was just in fun?
8. experimented with ESP, telepathy, or wished you were psychic?
9. been to anyone who practices "spirit-healing?"
10. sought healing through Christian Science?
11. tried to locate missing persons or objects by consulting someone with psychic powers?
12. tried to levitate an object by concentrating?
13. practiced automatic writing?
14. done water witching?
15. worn power beads or a rabbit's foot or any other kind of charm for protection, power, or blessing?
16. practiced any kind of black magic?
17. had in your library any books on metaphysics, astrology, self-realization, ESP, clairvoyance, New Age dream symbols, the I-Ching, the "ascended masters," the Akashic Records, the Essene Gospel of Peace, or any other occult, New Age or eastern mystical topics?

18. taken marijuana or LSD?
19. had in your house or possession any occult objects, pendants, or any items used in pagan worship?

There are many more, but I think you understand the principle. If you think of some others not mentioned here, renounce them before God to be free of their influence. As you study your Bible, you will come across many scriptures dealing with this subject. After you have renounced these involvements, command any demonic power in Jesus' name to depart from you. It is important to bind the demons in Jesus' name, asking that they be permanently removed forever. You will need to stand in faith over what has taken place.

Jesus wants us to be without any spot or wrinkle. Ultimately, it is He who makes us righteous, but by renouncing the "hidden works of darkness," you will make much greater strides in your spiritual life. Call each individual occult involvement sin, for that is what the Bible calls it. The Bible actually explains that Jesus came to destroy all *"the works of the devil"* (1 John 3:8). Be sure to burn or rid yourself of any occult, New Age, metaphysical, or Far Eastern spiritual occult objects or books. Ask God to fill those empty areas of your life with His Holy Spirit. You might pray a prayer like this:

Lord Jesus, I surrender my whole entire being to You— body, soul, and spirit. Please cleanse me from every past wrongful involvement and fill me now with your Holy Spirit that I may know you fully.

Once you are free, you have the responsibility not to let those demons return. Be sure to repent of any repeated sin until you have the total victory over that area of your life.

Jesus never gets tired of forgiving, but those who are spiritually reborn will have an inner aversion toward some of the things they once enjoyed. You must study the Scriptures and pray daily to stay close to God. Keep certain scriptures on hand that deal with your own specific problem areas so that you can use the Word of God effectively in your life. This is how Jesus responded when He was tempted by the devil during His wilderness experience on this earth. He did not try to defeat him with logical reasoning; rather, He defeated him by applying the Scriptures. If we focus on the light, we will become brighter. Opening a dark box in a bright room does not cause the room to darken, it removes the darkness and allows the light to enter! Remember, calling on the holy name of Jesus and His blood, as well as regularly and increasingly entering the Father's glory realm through praise and worship, have awesome power to protect you from any demonic onslaughts. Dear reader, may God lead you into an ever deeper knowledge of Him.

THE NAME OF GOD
Calling on Jesus

"They shall see His face, and His name shall be on their foreheads" (Revelation 22:4).

"Behold, the virgin shall be with child, and bear a Son, and they shall call His name Immanuel, which is translated, 'God with us'" (Matthew 1:23).

"...And His name will be called Wonderful, Counselor, Mighty God, Everlasting Father, Prince of Peace" (Isaiah 9:6).

"...but these are written that you may believe that Jesus is the Christ, the Son of God, and that believing you may have life in His name" (John 20:31).

"Nor is there salvation in any other, for there is no other name under heaven given among men by which we must be saved" (Acts 4:12).

"He had a name written that no one knew except Himself. He was clothed with a robe dipped in blood... His name is called The Word of God" (Revelation 19:12-13).

"Therefore God also has highly exalted Him and given Him the name which is above every name..." (Philippians 2:9).

"And Jesus answering them began to say: Take heed that no one deceives you. For many will come in My name, saying, 'I am He,' and will deceive many" (Mark 13:5-6).

"*For whoever calls on the name of the LORD shall be saved*" (Romans 10:13).

"*I will leave in your midst a meek and humble people, and they shall trust in the name of the LORD*" (Zephaniah 3:12).

"*Our help is in the name of the LORD, Who made heaven and earth*" (Psalm 124:8).

"*And it shall come to pass That whoever calls on the name of the LORD shall be saved*" (Acts 2:21).

"*Because he has set his love upon Me, therefore I will deliver him; I will set him on high, because he has known My name*" (Psalm 91:14).

"*The name of the LORD is a strong tower; the righteous run to it and are safe*" (Proverbs 18:10).

ABOUT THE AUTHOR

Joe and Vail Carruth

As a teenager Vail Carruth experimented with the Ouija board, astrology, psychic phenomena, and moved on to LSD, pot, and Eastern mysticism while in her twenties. During this time she obtained a fine arts degree from the University of California at Berkeley and studied piano at the San Francisco Conservatory of Music.

In her quest for spiritual enlightenment, Vail studied to become an instructor of Transcendental Meditation under the Maharishi Mahesh Yogi in Fiuggi, Italy. God used a non-traditional approach to show her the way to a fulfillment and a peace that she never dreamt possible.

Vail has appeared on radio and television to share about her journey to find truth, and her story has been included in books by several authors. She is available to travel and speak, sharing her insights and personal story with diverse groups, large or small.

Vail may be contacted through her website www.living-light.net and by emailing her, vail@living-light.net. She welcomes feedback and would like to personally dialogue with anyone who is interested in learning more. Thank you for reading this book; we pray that God will use it to help many others.

END NOTES

1. John Piper, *Seeing and Savoring Jesus Christ* (Wheaton, Ill.: Crossway Books, 2001), p. 21.

2. *Maharishi, On the Bhagavad-Gita*: A New Translation and Commentary *(Baltimore: Penguin Books, 1967), p. 18.*

3. *Maharishi, On the Bhagavad-Gita*, p. 226.

4. Robert Windquist, Affidavit of Dr. Robert N. Bellah filed in *Malnak versus Maharishi*, Civil Action no. C-76-341 in United States District Court for the District of New Jersey.

5. Maharishi, telephone interview in Brussels on November 30, 1975, Spiritual Counterfeits Project research files.

6. Pam Porter, *"Dodging the Yogic Fliers,"* Newsweek, July 17, 2000, p. 26.

7. *Maharishi, On the Bhagavad-Gita*, p. 224.

8. Dr. Frank Young, Chiropractor of the Year, unpublished letter about spine healing.

9. Tommy Tenney, *The God Chasers* (Shippensburg, PA: Destiny Image Publishers, Inc., 1998), p. 35.

10. William Jefferson, *The Story of the Maharishi* (New York: Pocket Books, 1976), p. 35.

11. John Paul Jackson, *Streams Newsletter*, May 2003.

12. Colin Martindale, *"Creative People: What Makes Them So Different,"* Psychology Today, July 1975, p. 50.

13. Merv Griffin, broadcast discussion about a drug offender sentenced to TM, Merv Griffin Show, April 1975.

14. Anonymous, *"The Enlightened Sentencing Project,"* a website dedicated to Maharishi's mission: www.enlightenedsentencing.org (September 15, 2007)

15. David Haddon and Vail Hamilton (Carruth), *TM Wants You* (Grand Rapids, MI: Baker Book House, 1976), p. 128.

16. Maharishi, *On The Bhagavad-Gita*, p. 76.

17. Statement made during convocation of Globalists in San Francisco, CA, Sept. 14, 1994.

18. Pam Porter, *"And The Fit Shall Lead,"* Atlanta Gazette, April 2, 1995, p. 17.

19. *Maharishi, On The Bhagavad-Gita*, pp. 4, 18.

20. Pam Porter, *"And The Fit Shall Lead,"* p. 17.

21. William Gibson, *A Season in Heaven* (Toronto, CA: Bantam Books, 1975), p. 104.

22. Anonymous, *"Who is This Man and What Does He Want?"* Spiritual Counterfeits Project paper, 1976, p. 4.

23. Gwen Shaw, *Unconditional Surrender*, (Jasper, AR: Engeltal Press, 1986), p.192.

24. *Maharishi, Meditations, The Science of Being and Art of Living*, rev. ed. (Los Angeles: International SRM Publications, 1967), p. 123-124.

AUTHENTIC ENLIGHTENMENT

RETAIL BOOK ORDER FORM

Please send me _____ copies of *Authentic Enlightenment* at $15.95 per copy. Add for postage and handling to **each address**: $2.00. These rates do not apply outside the United States. Arkansas residents must add $1.16 sales tax. Or you may order it through www.living-light.net.

TOTAL ENCLOSED $_____

NAME _____

ADDRESS _____

CITY _____

STATE/ZIP _____

Please make all checks and money orders payable to:
   Vail Carruth / Living Light (U.S. Funds Only)

Mailing Address:
   Vail Carruth / Living Light
   P.O. Box 721
   Lavaca, AR 72941
   USA

Email: vail@living-light.net

Bookstores and other wholesalers should order through Deeper Revelation Books www.deeperrevelationbooks.org or a distributor carrying this title.

Raised from the Dead,
A True Account

After a horrible car accident, Richard Madison was pronounced dead-on-arrival. His family was told three times to make funeral arrangements. God revealed Himself to Richard through an out-of-body experience, and ten weeks later he walked out of a wheelchair. He is now a walking miracle testimony to thousands of people throughout the world that God's love can powerfully restore even the most hopeless lives. This amazing book will build your faith.

ISBN: 978-0-942507-43-0   **—Price: $13.95**

⟫⟫◈◆◈⟪⟪

Richard Madison is a full-time evangelist who travels the world to tell the remarkable story of how God raised him from his deathbed and completely delivered him from drugs and alcohol. Richard is a highly sought after speaker with a powerful healing and prophetic ministry. He and his family live in Oakman, Alabama.

Richard L. Madison

"Jesus walked into that hospital room, and laid His hand on Rick Madison's head and healed him."   —Pat Robertson

"Fast living led to a dead end, but a new life began with an out-of-body experience."   —Ben Kinchlow

"Richard, you've had everything go wrong that could go wrong and...you are a living miracle."   —Dr. Kenneth Sharp
Vanderbilt University Medical Center

Our Glorious Inheritance
Volume Three
by Mike Shreve

The "OUR GLORIOUS INHERITANCE" eight volume series explores a powerful and edifying subject in God's Word: the revelation of over 1,000 names and titles God has given His people. Each name gives unique insight into a certain aspect of the total inheritance available to sons and daughters of God. Seeing the revelation of ALL of our names and titles provides the most comprehensive and complete view of our spiritual identity—who we are and what we possess as children of God.

In Volume Three, over 150 wonderful and inspiring names for God's people are explored, including: the Anointed of the Lord, the Blessed of the Father, Children of the Kingdom, Heirs of the Kingdom, God's Garden, Good Ground, Good Seed, Good Soldiers, the Just, Peacemakers, the Poor in Spirit and Trees of Righteousness. Get ready for a transformational experience!

ISBN: 978-0-942507-54-6   **—Price: $17.95**

To place an order for any of these books, send the amount of each book plus $5.00 s/h per book:

Deeper Revelation Books
P.O. Box 4260
Cleveland, TN 37320-4260

You may also order online:
www.deeperrevelationbooks.org or call: 1-423-478-2843

Revealing "the deep things of God"

	QTY	PRICE	AMOUNT
IN SEARCH OF THE TRUE LIGHT			
RAISED FROM THE DEAD			
OUR GLORIOUS INHERITANCE (VOL. THREE)			
(Add $5.00 s/h per book)	TOTAL AMOUNT		